A Biblical Perspective of God's Destiny for your Life

Kay Blugh Gaymes

ISBN: 978-1-907188-404

ISBN: 9781907188404

CONTENTS

Foreword

It was a great delight reading your book. I was blessed, challenged, refreshed, encouraged and inspired.

I believe 'Labour Pains' is a must read for every believer who is perplexed, confused, wearied and discouraged by the process of conceiving, carrying, birthing and developing a vision, a miracle or a destiny.

The body of Christ needs this book.

Well done and thank you.

Dr. David Okumgba

Acknowledgement

I want to thank God the Father Almighty, His blessed Son Jesus Christ and the power of the Holy Spirit, for directing me through the writing of this book. I was led through many passages of Scripture, and given much revelations and inspirations, as I sat at the computer for days and nights. It was not an easy task but I thank God for His grace and His strength in this accomplishment.

I especially want to give recognition for the credence to several Editions of **'The Word for Today'** written by Bob and Debby Gass with Ruth Gass Halliday, which assisted me in some Scripture references, and other guidance.

I want to thank my family for their encouragement that was necessary to buoy me on, and my friend Noreen Haynes for her loyal devotion in vetting this literature. I wish to thank Saeed Kydd for his contribution of the cover and images. I also want to thank my brothers, sisters and friends in the Lord who upheld me in their prayers and gave me their unswerving support, I esteem you highly. The Lord will reward you richly for standing behind me.

I hope that this book would have a positive impact in turning many lives around, inspiring them to come to know the Lord Jesus as their Saviour and to live fulfilled lives. My prayer also is that Christians would be challenged to live successfully by fulfilling God's plan, purpose, and calling for their lives. I rejoice with the young lady in New York who got pregnant after reading the first edition of this book. The doctor said she could not get pregnant but her faith was brought to life and God performed a miracle. There were others whose marriages were restored and other miracles took place.

If you know of someone who has been going through some struggles, please purchase a copy for him/her so that he/she would have an understanding that the days of miracles are not over.

Introduction

Each of us has been placed on this earth to fulfill a plan and purpose designed by God our Maker and has been endowed with particular gifts and talents to become successful in this life. However, the enemy has his agenda and that is to ensure we do not complete our assignments that God wants us to accomplish in order to fulfill our destiny. We have to be determined and willing to fight against the forces of hell, especially the spirit of fear, by using our spiritual weapons in order to succeed.

"For I know the plans I have for you," declares the Lord "plans to prosper you and not to harm you, plans to give you hope and a future… Then you will call upon me and come and pray to me, and I will listen to you. You will seek me and find me when you seek me with all your heart. I will be found by you…" Jeremiah 29:11-14 NIV.

The Word of God is our spiritual compass and road map. There are many examples of the lives of patriarchs, judges, priests, prophets and even kings, written for our learning. We just need to follow the good deeds or to take heed and avoid the consequences of the bad. The Word of God gives guidance, and we must depend on it for our sustenance and allow the Holy Spirit to help us discern the cunning devices of the enemy.

The journey of life can be a challenging and difficult venture. We would make mistakes, but we can make it successfully if we persevere, pursue, prepare and declare the will of God in our lives. We would encounter pain, pressure and suffering but God will give us the grace and strength to come out victoriously.

'Labour Pains' is a Biblical perspective and concept of fulfilling your visions, dreams and destiny in life. You can make it because Jesus fought and won the battle on your behalf and the power of the Holy Spirit makes it all possible.

THE VERSIONS OF THE BIBLE USED:

- The Living Bible (TLB)
- King James Version (KJV)
- New King James Version (NKJV)
- The Amplified Bible (AMP)
- New American Standard (NAS)
- New International Version (NIV)

New Living Translation (NLT)

Chapter 1

FAITH FIGHTS FEAR

What has Life offered you?

God wants you to know that no matter what the circumstances are in your life right now, the Word of God can impact positively upon you, as you read the pages of this book. Paul writes: ***'My dear children, for whom I am again in pains of childbirth until Christ is formed in you, how I wish I could be with you now…I am perplexed with you!'*** (Galatians 4:19, 20 NIV). It does not matter your age, colour, race or gender, God can turn things around for you. God knows the experience required to produce the character of Christ in you and He will do what ever it takes to bring it about. You may be experiencing some difficulties right now but God is faithful, He wants to bring you to the place where you will give birth to His plan, dreams and visions for your life. Let us take this spiritual journey with Christ and Be Blessed!

Has life been unkind to you from childhood until now? Were you ear-marked to become a doctor, nurse, lawyer, preacher, secretary, politician, or a philanthropist, teacher, or some other great profession? Was your family depending on you but it did not happen? Did you not even come close to their dreams because of some misfortune? Were there other issues, an accident, broken marriage, academic failures, and financial disaster? All sorts of disappointments can take place in life. The pain that emerges from any such situations can leave you so broken hearted. Sometimes you are thinking, why were you born, or where did you go wrong, or will you ever bounce back? But as the saying goes, 'Only God alone knows.'

On the other hand, some folks have had it 'all made' in life. They did not have to fight to achieve their success; it came so easy because it was already tailor-made. Or better still, they were 'born with a gold or silver spoon in their mouth'; being born in the perfect family, or endowed with the brain of a genius. The academics was a 'piece of cake', there was easy access to finance, life was perfect, they went through life with flying colours, then suddenly it happened, the rug was pulled from under their feet. It was like a nightmare and they are thinking they might not be able to shake themselves back to their former position; how they wish they would wake up out of this terrible dream. What's worst, the reality hits them, the party is over and all their friends have left, they are like the prodigal son. What was once so sweet has now turned bitter; they have lost it all, and just cannot figure out how it all happened.

Well, if you have been caught in the middle of any of these scenarios and you are about to throw in your towel, there is still hope, '*hope thou in the Lord*' (Psalm42:5). Do not give up, the difficulties that you have gone through in life were not meant to hurt you but to bring you to God's desired plan and purpose. When God takes something from your grasp, he is not punishing you, but merely opening your hands to receive something better. God has ear-marked you for greatness, if you thought that life was so wonderful before you fell like Humpty-Dumpty, God can put you back together again, so many times better than before. You only have to let go and let God do the remodeling of your life; the way He wants it.

God's plan for your life

We came into this world with God-given assignments, which are necessary to fulfill God's original plan and purpose for our lives. With these assignments come the ability to do our task and to do it well, ***'for it is God who is at work in you, both to will and to work for His good pleasure'*** (Philippians 2:13 NAS). Paul also states (Ephesians 2:10 NAS) ***'For we are His workmanship, .0created in Christ Jesus for good works, which God prepared beforehand, that we should walk in them.'*** We do not exist on earth by mere coincidence or human error. Maybe our parents thought they had an unplanned pregnancy, but God does not make any mistakes.

Satan's mission is to assign demons to derail us and to undermine the plans that God has for our lives; to demoralize and dehumanize the entire human race. He wants us to be failures and not to succeed; to encounter defeat, struggles, discouragement, and hardships. His intention is to counteract and eventually abort our God-given assignments and to make us miss out on God's purpose for our lives. Satan also uses people to carry out his agenda on nations and continents. So it is time for us to take the matter of our destiny seriously.

The word of God came to Jeremiah saying: ***"Before I formed thee in the belly I knew thee, sanctified thee and I have ordained thee as a prophet unto nations...Behold I have put my words in thy***

mouth. See, I have this day set thee over the nations and over the kingdoms, to root out, to pull down, to destroy, to throw down, to build and to plant" (Jeremiah 1: 5, 9 &10 KJV).

In Paul's letter to the Ephesians, he said ***"Moreover, because of what Christ has done we have become gifts to God that he delights in, for as part of God's sovereign plan we were chosen from the beginning to be His, and all things happen just as He decided long ago"*** (Ephesians1:11 TLB). Before you were born, God already had a plan for your life, so you were chosen and predestined according to that plan and God is working out everything that happens to you in life to conform to His will. As a matter of fact, He has His eyes on you and is designing your life so that He gets the honour and glory. However, the choice is yours, because He has made us free moral agents. There are times when He over rules by His power, as He did in Jonah's case when he refused to go down to Nineveh.

Sometimes, there can be an unrelenting battle between your flesh and your spirit, God's will and your way. In Romans 7:15- 25, Paul said ***"There is a war inside of me, I know that I should do good but it always turns out to be bad … it is sin inside of me that is stronger than I am that makes me do these evil things…Oh miserable man that I am. Who can deliver me from the torment of the flesh."*** We know that we can be delivered from the power of sin and death through the blood of Jesus Christ and by His resurrection power which makes us over-comers and victors, not victims; *for* ***'we can do all things through Christ who strengthens us'*** (Philippians 4:13) KJV.

Some people feel that they do not have what it takes to accomplish the will of God so they revert to going down the path which may appear to be easier; however, it may not be the right path for them. It is easier for a fish to follow the current down the river since it does not require much skill and energy, rather than to swim upstream against the current, which is much more strenuous, but has a lot more advantage and greater rewards. The fact of the matter is, the devil uses divisive means to get you to follow his plan, but you need to stick to God's plan.

It is recorded in Matthew 25: 14-30 (KJV& TLB), Jesus' story of the talents. A man who was going into another country had called his servants together. To one, he gave five talents, to another he gave two, and to another he gave one, according to their ability. The one who received five went immediately and bought and sold, resulting in him profiting by another five talents; the one that received two also went and worked and gained two more; but the one that received one went and dug in the ground, and hid the master's money.

The "man" came back after a long time and the servants each gave a report. The master praised the first for the good work and said to him, "You have been faithful in handling this small amount, so now I will give you many more responsibilities. Begin the joyous task I have assigned you." To the second he said "Good work, you are a good and faithful servant. You have been faithful with this small amount, now I will give you much more." The third man said to him, "I knew thee that thou art a hard man, and I was afraid you would rob me of what I earned, so I hid your money in the earth and here it is!"

The master replied, "Wicked man! Lazy slave! Since you knew I would demand your profit, you should at least have put my money in the bank, so I could have some interest". Taking the money from this man he gave it to the man with the five talents. "For the man who uses well what he has will be given more, and he shall have abundance. But the man who is unfaithful, what little responsibility he has shall be taken from him, and he shall be thrown as the useless servant out into outer darkness: there shall be weeping and gnashing of teeth."

It was a defining moment which gave each of them the chance to test their skills, develop initiative, practice good judgment and profit from their investment. The first two men did that by doubling up on what the master gave them but the third man was afraid of failing, so he buried his talent. We too shall receive responsibility and rewards according to how we operate in this life, so let us not waste our talents and time because our hard work will pay off or benefit us not in this life only but in the life to come.

Fight fear

One of the elements which may prevent you from fulfilling your potential, dreams, goals and ambitions in life, is the element of fear. Fear has torment (1John 4:18 NKJ). Your fears can actually immobilize you and prevent you from operating in confidence from our Lord, which comes from a dedicated life in Jesus Christ. You have to be bold and strong and be vigilant because your adversary walks about seeking whom he may devour. ***'For God has not given you a spirit of fear but of power and of love and of a sound mind'*** (11Timothy 1:7). Do not allow fears to erode your mental, emotional and physical power, thus destroying your purpose in God. God is saying ***"Fear not, for I am with you. Do not be dismayed. I am your God. I will strengthen you; I will help you; I will uphold you with my victorious right hand"*** (Isaiah 41:10).

Fear is the result of lack of confidence in God. We must counteract fear with faith and good courage. Faith is simply defined as active belief in God through a life of obedience. Courage on the other hand, is not the absence of fear, but the boldness to act in the presence of fear. Faith is like a mustard seed when being planted; it takes root and begins to grow, thus making your prayer for example, more effective. When we grow and develop such faith, we can see greater things happen as we extend our faith.

Jesus said, a mustard seed is the smallest seed, however when it is sown, it becomes the largest tree in the garden. The application of the analogy is thus: like a mustard seed, faith has the potential to rise to any mountainous situation and overcome it. Every challenge is not the same; varying levels of faith are required for varying levels of challenges. However, your faith will grow in dimensions, as time and challenges progress in life, and as God allows you to go through your storms of life, you should be grounded and rooted in the Word of God, thus enabling your faith to increase.

Let us look back at David while he was guarding his sheep. A lion and a bear came to attack his father's sheep, he could have been stricken with fear, but he smote them. He took the lamb from the lion and the bear in the strength of the Lord, and conquered them (1Samuel 17: 34-36 KJV). When the opportunity came afterwards for him to defeat Goliath, he could not use Saul's armour because he had never used anything like it before, he preferred to use what he was familiar with; sling shot and stones. David was able to conquer Goliath because his experience with God developed his faith and his courage and God led and guided him.

When David saw Goliath, he didn't stop to consider the odds or listen to the opinions of others, instead, he '…ran quickly toward the battle…to meet him' (1Samuel 17:48 NIV). He had confidence that his God would deliver him. When Goliath saw David he mocked him because he was just a young lad with a fair countenance. He thought that he could have just gotten rid of David in one swoop of his sword. David made a powerful confession saying, ***"You come against me with sword and spear and javelin, but I come against you in the name of the Lord Almighty, the God of the armies of Israel, whom you have defied"*** (1Samuel 17: 45 NIV). The velocity of the stone in that sling shot, and the power of God behind it caused the stone to land right in the middle of Goliath's forehead. Jesus is our conquering Lion of the Tribe of Judah, so give Him praise, honour and glory. He can conquer every giant and defeat every enemy in your life.

What is your weapon against fear when the enemy breathes out his venom and threats? We know he uses the mouths of all types of people in our lives to accomplish his schemes; it may be a family member, a friend, a foe, a co-worker or even a boss. We need to know the mind of God so that we can be over-comers and conquerors. Are you allowing the devil to manipulate, intimidate, malign, or undermine your confidence, bringing with it a spirit of fear which retards your progress? Fear of people, fear of failure and fear of rejection can tempt you to bury your gift. Speak the Word of God into your life, which will combat fear, so be courageous.

The prophet Isaiah says ***"Strengthen your weak hands, and confirm the feeble knees. Say to them that are of a fearful heart, be strong, and fear not: behold your God will come with a vengeance, even God with a recompense; He will come and save you."*** (Isaiah 35:3-4KJV)

There is a typical example of an enemy breathing out threats and the response to fear, recorded in Isaiah 36 (NIV). During the fourteenth year of King Hezekiah, Sennacherib, King of Assyria, fought against the cities that had little or no defense and defeated them with his strong army. Through these victories he felt as though he had enough power to conquer every territory in the region. He was well organized and boasted of his weapons and military might. He sent his mouth champion, Rabshakeh from Lachish to Jerusalem to King Hezekiah with a great army to boast. He stood at a strategic position at the water source of the upper pool, where he knew he would have a lot of attention and three of King Hezekiah' subjects; Eliakim, Shebna and Joah came to hear what he had to say.

He boasted, "Our great King of Assyria asks your King Hezekiah, what he bases his confidence on? You say you have strategy and military strength, but you speak only empty words. On whom are you depending, that you rebel against me? You are trusting in Egypt to help but they are a broken reed for a staff, and if you lean on them they will break, and the broken pieces will pierce a man's hand and wound him, as this has happened to other nations before!"

You may be saying, "I am trusting in the Lord our God, but it is God's high places and altars Hezekiah took away." (Hezekiah had broken down groves and idols in the temple when he started his reign, so his statement was not true). "He is now saying that Judah and Jerusalem shall worship before the altars. Now I am asking that you pledge to me so that I can go back to my master and king and I will give you two thousand horses and you can set riders on them. This is an offer which is too good to be true, you cannot turn it down and trust in chariots and horsemen from Egypt. The Lord has even given me instruction to say 'Go up and destroy the land' (this is also untrue) although I came without the Lord."

This guy Rabshakeh has an audacity which is unbelievable. Does this sound familiar though? The devil is a liar from the beginning and the father of many lies. His job is to defame and derail us and to make us lose our confidence in God, thinking that we can put our trust in man but man will fail us. The enemy likes to use all sorts of bait to entice us to join forces with him and make us think we are hearing from God. He offers false benefits which only disappear into bubbles and put us into all sorts of trouble.

Is there someone in your life that the enemy has been using to taunt you, make you afraid, or overpower you? When you hear the person's voice, do you buckle up and freeze with fright? The negative things he has been saying to you prevent you from operating according to God's schedule and calendar because of his controlling spirit. You feel helpless and are afraid to challenge him because what comes out of his mouth scares you, as he plays back the record of your past; you are so scared to make a move, whether it is out of the environment or to gravitate towards your calling. The stringent measure placed upon your life makes you immobile and you think that there is no way out but there is.

We need to look at the ploy and strategy of Rabshakeh as he went on taunting them with his frightening threats of what his army can do, to get the people of Jerusalem to join forces with him and turn from Hezekiah. When one of King Hezekiah's subjects told Rabshakeh to speak to them in the Syrian language and not in the Jewish language that the people on the wall would not understand, he replied that his master had sent him to those men also, who were doomed with no sense of hope or vision. He said if they did not come on his side, they would live to eat their own dung and drink their own urine.

He further called out with a loud voice "Hear the words of the great King, the King of Assyria. Do not let Hezekiah deceive you. He cannot deliver you! Do not let Hezekiah persuade you to trust in the Lord when he says, 'The Lord will surely deliver you; this city will not be given into the hand of the king of Assyria.'"

He further went on "Make peace with me and come out to me. Then every one of you will eat from his own vine and fig tree and drink water from his own cistern, until I come and take you to a land like your own; a land of bread and vineyards. Has the god of any nation ever delivered his land from the hand of the King of Assyria?" (Isaiah 36: 13-18 NIV). He sounds just like the devil offering gifts, giving false hope to lure people into his traps, making their hearts fearful.

Do you think that God will allow you to go through a trial which you will not be able to withstand or a battle which He thinks you cannot fight and win? The Lord promises that He will make a way where there is no way. ***'When you go through deep waters and great trouble, I will be with you. When you go through rivers of difficulty you will not drown! When you walk through the fire of oppression, you will not be burned up - the flames will not consume you'*** (Isaiah 43:2 TLB).

The people remained silent and did not reply, which was King Hezekiah's command. The Bible warns ***'Have no fear of sudden***

disaster or of the ruin that overtakes the wicked, for the Lord will be your confidence and will keep your foot from being snared' (Proverbs 3:25-26 NIV). We are not to panic when we hear of bad news, although we do it most of the times. Panic makes us find it difficult to breathe; we lose our ability to stay calm and keep our composure. Our palms become wet with perspiration; we are jittery when we become overwhelmed with fear but we need to breathe the name of Jesus. Sometimes we feel as if we will lose our minds in the midst of a disaster and that there is nothing anyone can say to us that makes much sense. It is in these circumstances that the grace and might of God will lead us where our mental capacity cannot take us.

The Word combats fear

In Genesis 3: 1-4 the devil speaking through the serpent spoke to Eve saying, "Did God really say, 'You must not eat from any tree of the garden'?" Eve clarifying the point said to the serpent "We may eat fruit from the trees of the garden, but God did say, we must not eat of the fruit from the tree that is in the middle of the garden, and we must not touch it, or we will die." The serpent replied "You will not surely die, for God knows that when you eat of it your eyes will be opened, and you will be like God, knowing good and evil." We know that Eve ate the fruit and gave it to her husband Adam. They both disobeyed God and were cast out of the Garden of Eden. This brought sin and death upon all mankind.

The devil offers: lying trade offs, disillusions, illusive dreams and financial frustrations, which undermine our trust in God, make us lose our joy, our hope, our peace, and even make us doubt what God has said to us. We sometimes experience barriers in communication with God when we cannot even pray and read the Word effectively. Eve spoke the word which God said, but she lacked the authority and the willpower to act on it. **We must speak**

in clarity and with authority to the devil and ward off his attacks and threats. When we speak the Word of God with authority the enemy's actions are paralyzed because there is power in the Word of God.

Jesus' example to us: being full of the Holy Spirit was led by the Spirit in the desert, where for forty days He was tempted by the devil. He ate nothing during those days, and at the end of them He was hungry. The devil told Jesus, if he was the Son of God, tell this stone to become bread, but Jesus answered him *"It is written: **'Man does not live on bread alone'**"*. The devil further led him up to a high place and showed him all the kingdoms of the world and told him he will give him all authority and splendour, for it has been given to him and he can give it to anyone he wanted to, if He would worship him. Jesus answered, *"It is written: **'Worship the Lord your God and serve Him only.'**"*

The devil further led Jesus to Jerusalem and had him stand on the highest point of the temple and told him to throw himself down. Satan said *"For it is written: 'He will command his angels concerning you to guard you carefully; they will lift you up in their hands, so that you will not strike your foot against a stone'"* (Luke 4: 9).

Jesus answered, "It says: ***'Do not put the Lord your God to the test'"*** (Luke 4:12NIV).

The power of God is in the word and the word is quick and sharper than any two-edged sword. We only have to use this weapon to cast down every imagination and every thought that lifts itself up above the knowledge of God. ***'Death and life are in the power of the tongue, and those who love it will eat its fruit'*** (Proverbs 18:21).

The name of Jesus brings serenity and peace to our heart. The devil wins the battle when we respond with fear after his threats. Take a minute to whisper a prayer, quote a verse of scripture, listen to inspiring music or talk to a Christian friend who would encourage you and one you can confide in. Franklin D. Roosevelt said "we have nothing to fear but fear itself."

Are you worn and burnt out?

When we examine some of the words that Rabshakeh breathed out, we would realize that they are some of the same words that the devil is still using to keep some people in captivity and in bondage of fear. They are afraid of advancing beyond what the enemy has been saying through their skeptics. When king Hezekiah heard the threats that Rabshakeh had breathed out, he rent his clothes, covered himself with sackcloth and went into the house of the Lord. He sent his subjects and the elders of the priests covered with sackcloth to Isaiah the prophet. It is important to note here their message to Isaiah, Hezekiah says:

"This day is a day of trouble and of rebuke and disgrace, for the children come to the point of birth and there is no strength to bring forth. It may be that the Lord your God will hear the words of Rabshakeh, whom his master, the king of Assyria, has sent to ridicule the living God, and that he will rebuke him for the words the Lord your God has heard. Therefore pray for the remnant that still survives" (Isaiah 37: 3-4 KJV). Even Hezekiah was fearful of the threats.

Are you worn out by hearing threats or negative remarks that leave you without strength to push yourself into your destiny? The strength that is used "in labour" which is necessary for bringing your dreams, hopes, plans, ideas, and visions to "a safe delivery", we somehow cannot find it. We are too timid; our knees are buckling because we are too stricken with fear to come through. The devil sometimes strips us of our courage and exposes us, maybe by even bringing up our past failure to embarrass us, he even laughs and mocks us. We are so distressed we can smell and sense the intensity of failure thus we draw back into our shell because we feel that we will never make it to success and fulfill God's purpose. There is no strength to come through; we say, 'It can never happen.'

All sorts of anxiety and stress are rushing to our minds, which seem to block our focus, rob us of our peace of mind. We never foresee these problems. We were doing the right things in life, but the enemy off-loads and dumps some stuff on us and we become desperate, almost to the point of being insane or giving up and wanting to throw in the towel. Right now, you are thinking it is impossible to tap into the resources of heaven, and heaven is certainly not in your view at this moment because all your problems seem like the rock of Gibraltar during this time of crisis.

The word of God encourages you today: ***"You are my servant; I have chosen you and have not rejected you. Do not fear, for I am with you; do not be dismayed, for I am your God. I will strengthen you and help you; I will uphold you with my righteous right hand. All who rage against you will surely be ashamed and disgraced; those who oppose you will be as nothing and perish. Though you search for your enemies, you will not find them. Those who wage war against you will be as nothing at all. For I am the Lord, your God, who takes hold of your right hand and says to you, do not fear; I will help you"(Isaiah41: 9-13 NIV).***

Many times when we are in trouble we run from God instead of running to Him. In the midst of adversity we freeze up and our human constitution does not have the ability to fight the forces of hell. We lose our trust in God, but never doubt in the dark what God told you in the light. ***"Without faith it is impossible to please God, because anyone who comes to Him must believe that …He rewards those who earnestly seek him"*** (Hebrews 11:6 NIV). Faith is developed by reading, hearing and filling your mind with the Scriptures. ***'Faith comes by hearing and hearing by the word of God'*** (Romans10:17).

'Do not cast your confidence away; it will be richly rewarded. You need to persevere so that when you have done the will of God, you will receive what he has promised' (Hebrews 10:35-36 NIV). ***'God is a very present help in time of trouble'*** (Psalm 46:1). When we hit a rough spot like Hezekiah did, our tendency is to feel as though the job is too big for God to handle, but this is when we should trust the Great God Jehovah as our everlasting strength. We are the object of his love and concern. Even when our vision gets blurred and our thinking fogs up, we look up and can't see Him clearly but He is there. Do not look at the size of your problem but look to the greatness of your God.

Let us apply to our lives the counsel that God spoke to Joshua in preparation to cross the river Jordon and to conquer the heathen nations:

"Be strong and courageous, because you will lead these people to inherit the land I swore to their forefathers to give them. Be strong and very courageous. Be careful to obey all the law my servant Moses gave you; do not turn from it to the right or to the left, that you may be successful wherever you go. Do not let this Book of the law depart from your mouth; meditate on it day and night, so that you may be careful to do everything written in it. Then you will be prosperous and successful. Have I not commanded you? Be strong and courageous, Do not be terrified; do not be discouraged, for the Lord your God will be with you wherever you go." (Joshua1: 6-9 NIV).

Be encouraged that God will always keep his side of the bargain, if you will only keep yours. Even when you are walking through the dark valley of death you will not be afraid, for God is close beside you; guarding and guiding you all the way. Maybe you have experienced a tragedy that has left you feeling indifferent about the future, or heartbreak, and you are still writhing in pain. You may try to rationalize it by telling yourself, "As long as I don't care, it won't hurt." The fear of being wounded again is very real; for a burned child dreads fire. You can't live the rest of your life in fear. God wants to revive your passion today and give you a future filled with hope so that you can face all your tomorrows. '***You will have courage because God will give you hope. You will take your time, and rest in safety'*** (Job 11: 18 TLB). Are you willing to let Him renew your desire and wipe out the pain of the past? He will! All you have to do is surrender to His love today and He'll do the remodeling of your life.

Chapter 2

DESIRES ARE DETERMINED BY DEPENDENCIES

I f your **desire** is to fulfill God's will for your life, and your **decisions** are **determined** by God who is your ultimate **dependency,** then all is well; but if your life is solely **dependent** on the world, the flesh and the devil, then your life is in **danger**. The words of Hezekiah have been re-echoing down the corridors of times. ***'This day is a day of trouble and frustration and blasphemy; it is a serious time, as when a woman is in heavy labour trying to give birth, and the child does not come*** (Isaiah 37:3 TLB). There are Man-kinds who were 'pregnant' with God's plan and purpose, started the process and were not able to develop to 'full-term' but 'aborted' the plan of God, while there are those who, with time, came to 'full maturation' went into labour (times of trials and tests) and eventually gave 'birth' to God's plan.

There are various cases that can occur in our lives as regards to the plan of God. Some people started out well and continued almost right through life and almost at the very end, for some strange reason just messed up the plan and failed. There can be a series of events that can account for certain adverse situations which may cause a man or woman to fall short of the will of God for their lives. Some had a bad start but repented and finished the course well while some kept on falling and Jesus kept right on redeeming because He is our Redeemer. There are others who began well and made it with flying colours to the very end. Which category will you like to find yourself in? Some of these examples are found in the Word of God that we can learn from.

There are different guidelines which you must follow, during your pregnancy with God's plans for your life. This conception is as a result of the intimacy between you and God. It is therefore vital for you to allow God to take care and develop you properly, so that you can come forth and deliver at full term. You may be in a delicate season of your life and you have to carry that pregnancy or dream with utmost care. A pregnant person has to be a disciplined person, which means having a proper diet, taking the supplements, making sure that you have regular doctor check-ups etc. but you have to stick to the plan to avoid complications. This principle which holds true for the physical can also be applied to the spiritual. This means reading the Bible, praying, having fellowship with the body of Christ to name a few.

The Lord declares: ***"For I know the plans I have for you, plans to prosper you and not to harm you, plans to give you hope and a future. Then you will call upon me and come and pray to me. And I will listen to you. You will seek me and find me when you seek me with all your heart. I will be found by you...*** "(Jeremiah 29: 11-14 NIV). Stick to the plan.

When you are pregnant you are uncomfortable at times. You can be in God's plan yet at times you feel overwhelmed and encumbered. The period looks so long, you get tired and fed-up, you wish you could skip some stages and seasons of the journey and just reach your destination. The uneasy feelings of sickness or discomfort cause you to be discouraged; a slip or an accident can cause you to abort your dream. If you don't stick to the plan, so many uneventful things can happen, however you should try not to abort God's plan. Paul said it so beautifully for us:

'But we have this treasure in jars of clay (our inner beings) to show that this all-surpassing power is from God and not from us. We are hard pressed on every side, but not crushed; perplexed, but not in despair; persecuted, but not abandoned; struck down, but not destroyed. We always carry around in our body the death of Jesus, so that the life of Jesus may also be revealed in our body.' (2 Corinthians 4: 7-10 NIV)

You may be down today; flat on your face, can't even lift your head, but God is not finished with you yet, he will resuscitate you, pick you up, dust you off and give you the strength and will to start again, but you have to call on him. God is saying ***"Call upon me and I will answer you, and I will tell you great and mighty things, which you do not know"*** (Jeremiah 33:3). Jesus is saying ***"Cast your cares on me for I care for you."*** You may say "No I have gone too far." Is it because you may have fallen in sin? If so, then repent, get your hopes back up again, God has a back up plan, He did it for Samson, David and others and He can do it for you.

You may think that God is so disappointed in you that you are afraid to talk to him; as though he has a big stick ready to beat you, 'No, He is a loving God'. You think that you have surprised God when you failed; guess what, you did not, He knew it before that you would fail, but he trusted you and is still trusting you, so come on think like the prodigal son and return to the Father.

Whatever you are going through right now, irrespective of the season or the test; it may be a time of despair, discouragement or a back-sliding condition; the enemy wants you worn out, or even dead. You may have a **problem** but God has a **promise**. Find it in the Word! It may be only a matter of time when God will reveal his **purpose,** look out for your spiritual or financial **prosperity.** No matter what happens, don't abort the **plan,** God may be just about to fulfill His **prophetic** manifestations through you or in you.

Additionally, you have been hand-picked by God for His purpose; He has too much invested and deposited in you already to let you go to the enemy. When Jesus told a young man once to follow Him, the young man said, "Allow me to bury my father first." Jesus responded, "Let the dead bury their dead." You might have to forsake some relationship, old habit, some addiction, even your own personal agenda, in order to put things in the right **perspective**. This decision is vital so that you can continue to **pursue** your goals and desires in Jesus Christ.

Samson - God's plan or not?

I would like to bring to your attention, the life of Samson as an outstanding example of one who was destined with a plan to liberate and deliver the Israelites from the Philistines as recorded in the Book of Judges 13-16. The Bible said that the children of Israel did evil again in the sight of the Lord and the Lord delivered them into the hand of the Philistines for forty years. Manoah of the family Danites, along with his wife was barren, and bore no child. The angel of the Lord appeared unto the woman and said to her:

"You are sterile and childless, but you are going to conceive and have a son. Now see to it that you drink no wine or other fermented drink and that you do not eat anything unclean, because you will conceive and give birth to a son. No razor may

be used on his head, because the boy is to be a Nazirite, set apart to God from birth, and he will begin the deliverance of Israel from the hands of the Philistines." (Judges 13: 3-5 NIV)

If we examine this closely, many times in the Bible when God is about to bring His purpose into existence, the woman He is about to use to bring forth this plan, is barren or childless. Let us imagine that you are about to hear God's plan for you through an angel because God is about to change your barren or stagnant state in life to a life of hope and friutfulness. Fulfillment is about to come to you and your status will change from poverty to prosperity, from struggle to stability.

There are however, some conditions to it, the terms may not be the full-term Nazarite vow, but you are about to hear such words as 'Come out from among them and be separated, touch not the unclean thing and I will be your God and you shall be my next chosen vessel.' God is looking for someone on whom He can depend, and who will obey His Word at any cost and place faith and trust in Him, despite the circumstances or situation.

Let us reflect on the life of Samson who was destined to become a deliverer. The woman gave birth to a boy and named him Samson. He grew and the Lord blessed him, and the Spirit of the Lord began to stir within him. He went down to Timnah and saw a young Philistine woman. When he returned, he said to his father and mother, "I have seen a Philistine woman in Timnah; now get her for me as my wife." His father and mother asked him if he had to go to the uncircumcised Philistine to get a wife. His answer was, "Get her for me, she's the right one for me." His parents did not know that this was from the Lord, who was seeking an occasion to confront the Philistines: for at that time the Philistines had dominion over Israel (Judges 14: 4).

There are times when God is leading us to do unprecedented things, which we do not understand but we can sense the Holy Spirit's leading and prodding. Some people would not understand what God is doing in our lives, not even our relatives but it is important that we obey. Samson went with his parents to Timnah and suddenly a young lion came roaring toward him. The Spirit of the Lord came upon him in power so that he tore the lion apart with his bare hands as he might have torn a kid, but he did not tell his parents what he did.

The power of the Holy Spirit is to defeat the attacks of the enemy**. *'When the enemy comes in like a flood the Spirit of the Lord will lift up a standard against him'*** (Isaiah 59:19 KJV). When we cannot make it in our strength, we should call upon God through His Son Jesus Christ. Jesus makes the intercession for us through God the Father, and the Holy Spirit does the work in us. The Triune Being works in unity!

He then went and talked with the woman and he liked her. He later went back and married her. On his way he turned aside to look at the lion's carcass. In it was a swarm of bees and some honey, which he scooped out with his hands and ate as he went along. When he rejoined his parents, he gave them some, and they ate it. But he did not tell them that he had taken the honey from the lion's carcass.

God will bring honey out of a situation in which the enemy had meant to destroy your life. The process that God would use to bring the victory may be slow, but you need only to ask God for the patience and to wait and see the outcome. You can take note also that Samson kept some things from his parents. There are some things that we need to keep silent about. It was said about Mary, Jesus' mother ***'But Mary kept all these things, and pondered them in her heart'*** (Luke 2:19); she did not share every thing. Not every one will believe your story or understand what you are trying to say, but God is working behind the scenes.

When they came together to have a wedding feast, Samson was given thirty companions, to whom he put forward a riddle; if they did not solve it, they were to give him thirty linen garments and thirty sets of clothes. The riddle was: “Food came out of the eater and sweetness from the strong!” For three days they could not figure the answer out, so they went to his wife, for her to get the answer out of her husband, threatening to burn her and her father’s household to death. She then went to Samson and begged him until she got the answer from him.

On the seventh day they were able to give the answer to Samson. He made an interesting comment “If you had not plowed with my heifer, you would not have solved my riddle,” meaning if they had not manipulated and threatened his wife they would not have known the answer to the riddle. There are times the enemy gets us to do things and make compromises that God does not desire. We have to be wise in our decision-making and be careful with whom we align our allegiances. Samson’s wife’s allegiance was with his enemy and not with him.

Samson then went and struck down thirty Philistines, stripped them of their clothes and took them to his wife to give to these men. God was about to use Samson in various ways, e.g. when the Philistines were waiting on him to ambush him, Samson waited until midnight, got up, and took the gate and the two posts of the city of Gaza and went away with them on his shoulder, bars and all.

He then loved a woman in the valley of Sorek, her name was Delilah. The Lords of the Philistines came to her and advised that she must entice him to find out where his strength lay, to see by what means they could prevail against him, that they may bind him and afflict him. They promised to give her eleven hundred pieces of silver. It can be so easy for some folks to betray a close friend by just buying them out. Judas was paid thirty pieces of silver to betray the Lord Jesus. You would remember the story, where Samson mocked her three times, telling her lies about his strength but she did not give up. She entreated him daily with her sweet talk until his soul was vexed to death.

You may wonder why Samson did not run away; you would think that he was witty enough to recognize that Delilah was undermining him because each time he tricked her she had the Philistines waiting to take him out. Did his ego make him stick around, because it would be cowardice for him to run from a woman? Was he playing the role of a macho man? Or was this the plan of God? His soul could not take any more of her pleas; eventually he gave in, telling her his heart, and ended up telling her everything. Are you telling the wrong person everything about your life, someone who can destroy you and tear your soul apart? Be careful, this can be a dangerous game you are playing.

"No razor has ever been used on my head because I have been a Nazirite set apart by God since birth. If my head were shaved, my strength would leave me, and I would become as weak as any other man" (Judges 16:17 NIV). When Delilah saw that he had told her everything, she sent word to the rulers of the Philistines, "Come back once more; he has told me everything." So the rulers of the Philistines returned with the silver in their hands. Putting him to sleep on her lap, she called a man to shave off the seven braids of his hair, and so began to subdue him. And his strength left him, (Judges 16:18 NIV).

To answer the question as to whether it was a set up by God or not, it was not! James said ***"Let not man when he is tempted say he is tempted by God, for God tempts no man."*** There's no way a temptation to sexual sin can be called a trial sent from God. He doesn't test our faith by setting us up to sin. His weakness was women and it eventually caused his downfall. Jesus gives us strength over all the power of the enemy (Luke10:19). Paul says ***"I can do all things through Christ who strengthens me"*** (Philippians 4:13 NAS). It is so easy to give in to the flesh, to bend backwards to please a man or a woman, not knowing that the devil is the mastermind behind all these schemes and strategies.

There are so many Delilahs out there who are ready to get so many Samsons to destroy the plans of God, while there are some Samsons who would forsake the plan of God to go after some Delilahs. It is time for them to discern the trickery of the enemy, run for their lives and follow through with God's plan. ***'Be careful - watch out for attacks from Satan, your great enemy. He prowls around like a hungry, roaring lion, looking for some victim to tear apart. Stand firm when he attacks. Trust the Lord; and remember that other Christians all around the world are going through these sufferings too***' (1 Peter 5: 8, 9 TLB).

We read how Delilah told Samson that the Philistines were upon him and he awoke out of his sleep, thinking, "I'll go out as before and shake myself free" but he did not know that the Lord had left him. Sometimes we can lose our place in the will of God and do not even realize it. The Philistines seized him, gouged out his eyes and took him to Gaza. Binding him with bronze shackles; they set him to grinding in the prison. When we are out having fun in ways that do not please God we cannot see the end results. We don't even realize that the enemy has a death sentence on our lives or that he wants to enslave us and put us in shackles and chains.

Maybe you are a Christian who has fallen into the sin of adultery, fornication, homosexuality or some other sin and you are saying, "I will go out as before and shake myself free" at church where everyone is free to dance, sing, praise, pray or even preach but you do not know that the Lord has left you. You may be living an undercover or double standard life, but God sees through the thickest veil or a wall. It is only a matter of time when He would expose your sin. God is saying to you ***"I will judge each of you… and punish or reward each according to your own actions. Oh, turn from your sins while there is yet***

time. Put them behind you and receive a new heart and a new spirit. For why will you die? I do not enjoy seeing you die", the Lord God says. "Turn and live!" (Ezekiel 18: 30-32).

You may be saying, we are now living in the day of grace, not under the law but that is even worse. You are not excused: living under grace does not give you a license to sin. You cannot live your life anyhow you please because grace is not cheap. As a child of God, you are going to be held responsible and accountable. It cost God the death of His only Son; grace is God's unmerited favour, and we could not earn it or pay for it and He does not dispense it to any one unless they are 'born again'. We have to set the standards which are linked and lined up to the Word of God; He is depending on you to shine your light in this dark world so that others could come to know the Lord as their Saviour. Don't let Jesus down. He said ***"In this world you shall have tribulation: but be of good cheer; I have overcome the world"*** (John 16:33 KJV).

Don't forget the vow or the covenant when you find yourself in a mid-life crisis, a compromising situation, or when you just decide to feed the flesh alone and forget the spirit. When you break your vow or your covenant with God, then God is not obligated to stand by a broken vow although He is merciful. If you have been fulfilling the lust of the flesh and have walked away from God's original plan, cry out to Him today, He will take you back; He is waiting for you. You may feel that God has you in a vice today and you cannot get away. It is because He loves you too much to let you go.

In modern day business we can make purchases and there is full guarantee that if the commodity does not please us, we can send it back or take it back by a certain time and we receive all our money back. We sometimes apply this principle to marriages if our spouse does not please us we take her back or send him back because we are unhappy with the choice after a few days, months or years. Make certain you do not forfeit God's plan, especially if your marriage was ordained by God. Seek God's permission and His direction on your movements.

Having subdued Samson, it was victory time for the Philistines who assembled to celebrate and offer a great sacrifice to Dagon their god and to celebrate. When the people saw him, they praised their god, saying; "Our god has delivered our enemy into our hands, the one who lay waste our land and multiplied our slain." In their high spirit they shouted, "Bring out Samson to entertain us." So they called Samson out of the prison, and he performed for them. We can be a hero one day and be ridiculed the next. It does not take long for the enemy to bring us to nothing.

When they stood him among the pillars, Samson said to the servant who held his hand. "Put me where I can feel the pillars that support the temple, so that I may lean against them. The temple was crowded with men and women. All the rulers of the Philistines were there, and on the roof were about three thousand watching Samson perform. Then Samson prayed to the Lord, ***"O Sovereign Lord, remember me. O God, please strengthen me just once more, and let me with one blow get revenge on the Philistines for my two eyes."***

Samson then reached toward the two central pillars on which the temple stood; his hair was beginning to grow back. Bracing himself against them, his right hand on the one and his left hand on the other, he said "Let me die with the Philistines!" Then he pushed with all his might, and down came the temple on the rulers and all the people in it. Thus he killed many more when he died than when he was alive. Samson may not have lived a fulfilled life the way God had desired for him but he had time to repent and make a come back at the time of his death. Please don't wait until you are on your death bed to regret and repent, at that time it is too late for God to fulfill his destiny in your life, and therefore you would have had a wasted life.

God loves us in spite of

God sometimes disciplines us to keep us in check, less we fall out of line. You may be at the refiner's fire, God's fire, and it is burning away the impurities in order to refine you. ***'He will sit and closely watch as the dross is burned away. He will purify the Ministers of God, (or His children) refining them like gold or silver so that they will do their work for God with pure Hearts'*** (Malachi 3: 3). We may be feeling the intensity of the heat as it is being turned up, that's when we are at the stage of emerging as pure gold or silver. It is not easy but it is for our own good.

Or we may be like the clay in the potter's hand where we need to be yielded and moulded and fashioned by the potter, who is Jesus Christ. ***'When the vessel of clay is marred in the hand of the potter: so he made it again into another vessel, as seemed good to the potter'*** (Jeremiah 18:3-4). When the clay goes into heat, if there are impurities in the vessel, it cracks. The potter has to melt it and take out that unclean element which is causing the crack, mold it again and fashion it into his desired vessel and back into the heat it goes and emerges into that beautiful vessel that the potter desires. That is what God does with us when we have unclean elements: he has to break us, melt us, mold us and fashion us again.

God wants us to be more like Jesus, so that our experiences of temptation would be like that of Jesus. When He was tempted in the wilderness, He spoke the Word. We may experience rejection by family, the complexities of caring for others, criticism by religious folks, or being betrayed by those whom we love and have invested our life and time in. James says 'We make… mistakes' (James 3: 2), so we need to learn to forgive ourselves. There are lots of the times we are guilty of doing the wrong thing with the right motive.

Paul says ***"No…I am still not all I should be, but I am bringing all my energies to bear on this one thing: Forgetting the past and looking forward to what lies ahead"*** (Philippians 3:13 TLB). The memories of our past can be very painful and if we keep bringing them up they can influence our future. God is saying ***'Forget the former things; do not dwell on the past'*** (Isaiah 43:18 NIV), God does not bring them up so why should we.

Satan likes to afflict the children of God for several reasons. Maybe to get us to turn our backs on God, to discredit or lose confidence in Him but God wants us to stay in the fight. Paul went through some tough times and trials. A messenger of Satan was assigned to Paul to buffet him, he experienced blow after blow. Paul sought God to take away these trials; what he called 'a thorn in the flesh' but God's answer to him was, ***"My grace is sufficient for you, for my power is made perfect in weakness."*** Paul came to the conclusion then that he will gladly boast all the more, about his trials, so that Christ's power may rest on him (2Corinthians 12:9 NIV). We only need to see our pain, weaknesses and trials from God's perspective, just understand that He is working out every detail in our lives for His honour and glory, so give Him praise no matter what comes our way.

We were born with all sorts of weaknesses. They usually bring with them temptations but the positive side of this is; Paul says that ***'God is able to make you stand!'*** (Romans14:4). We can stand, not in our own strength but in the strength of Jesus Christ. By ourselves we cannot make it; we would just be an easy target for the enemy. We can stand in Christ for the plan of God for our life: so that we can regain our health, restoration of our marriage, for our finances to be replenished, success in our career and our education. Stand with Christ concerning the struggles of our flesh.

When we do the standing God does the strengthening; He will strengthen us over and over, again and again. It will not be easy, it can be very challenging facing the circumstances before us. Sometimes the memory comes back to haunt us; we are constantly reminded of our imperfect past, especially when there are some memories that are here to stay. It takes the grace of God to stand up to the fight the forces of hell by making the right decision to come back to the Father, in genuine repentance and prayer, also getting into the Word of God. We can stand if we really want to, so receive the grace of God to stand and move on. We just need to place our desires in God's hand because our dependency will determine our outcome.

We learn things about God when we are in trouble that we would not learn otherwise, because adversity drives us closer to Him. ***'The Lord is near to the broken-hearted, and saves those who are crushed in spirit'*** (Psalm 34:18 NAS). Jesus says we must cast all our cares upon Him for He cares for us. Adversity draws us closer to God, and problems force us to look to God and depend on Him instead of ourselves. Paul writes, ***"We…saw how powerless we were to help ourselves; but that was good, for then we put everything into the hands of God, who alone can save us…"*** (11Corinthians1:9 TLB).

Submitting the situation to God and trusting Him with His ways, means, and timing, is hard for most of us to do, because we like to be in control. God is still a loving Father who sent His son to die for our sins. Turn to Jesus and run for your life before the enemy put you in stocks and bonds, and dig out your eyes; making you spiritually blind or paralyzed or maybe eventually killing you. So seek God now. David in his repentance said, ***"It***

is a broken spirit you want, remorse and penitence. A broken and a contrite heart, O God, you will not ignore" (Psalm 51: 17 TLB).

Say this prayer with me:

Dear God and Father, through Jesus Christ, I repent today of my past failures. I have been doing my own thing for too long, hence I have made so many mistakes and now I have come to a dead-end in my life where I have to confess that I cannot go down the same path any more. I have made a mess of my life by taking the steering wheel and following my own intuition. I need to look to you for directions. For your word says, all things work together for good to those who love you, for those who are the called, according to your purpose. I bind fear, dismantle and nullify every strategy, plan, purpose, tactic, lie, and slander that the enemy has spoken to me. I defeat his ploys through the blood of Jesus Christ. Show me the way I ought to go. I am willing to trust you in every circumstance and situation in my life. I accept your challenges now, and I thank you Holy Spirit for your direction in Jesus' name, with thanksgiving. Amen.

Chapter 3

When Prayer Prevails

One of the requests that Hezekiah had for Isaiah after the threat of Rabshakeh was: "But perhaps the Lord your God heard the blasphemy of the king of Assyria's representative as he scoffed at the Living God. Surely God won't let him get away with this. Surely God will rebuke him for those words. Oh Isaiah, pray for us who are left!" (Isaiah 37: 4 TLB). Prayer is a vital link in the process of achieving God's plan for our lives. Just sitting and waiting for things to happen would not work. Jesus is saying to us ***"Ask, using my name, and you will receive, and your cup of joy will overflow"*** (John 16: 24 TLB). You have to superimpose your authority through Jesus Christ over every struggle, situation and trial that Satan has advanced towards you, through prayer. You have to gather up your shield of faith, your breastplate of righteousness and stand up for your destiny and purpose.

In a crisis, even those who would say they don't believe in God will pray secretly. During any turbulent time, as in the air when a plane finds itself in difficulty, passengers would begin to pray. Real need augurs and fuels prayer. We are very much aware now that ***'God is a present help in time of trouble'*** *(Psalm 46:1)*. We quickly come to the conclusion that we cannot handle many problems outside of the periphery of prayer, only God can resolve these issues. David, the man after God's own heart, said, ***"In the night His song shall be with me, and my prayer unto the God of my life"*** (Psalm 42:8). There are some prayers that are uttered at midnight when we turn into our beds and cannot sleep. We have no alternative but to cry out to God for help.

Our tears flow uncontrollably, we are so deeply hurt that only God can heal our sorrows and calm our fears. Our limp words are meant only for an infinite God to hear, not for human beings' ears because they won't understand. The fear is too deep; it causes us to stay awake as our bodies cringe and panic at the thought of tomorrow. The mixed feelings of rage and anxiety are too private to share even with our closest loved ones or relatives. We are afraid of the company of friends less we are tempted to share our deepest secret but we know that we have a High-priest who is touched with the feelings of our infirmities. The question that plagues us at times is; "Does God care?" The song writer says, 'Yes, He cares.'

1. Does Jesus care when my heart is pained,
Too deeply for mirth and song
As the burdens press, and the cares distress,
And the way grows weary and long

2. Does Jesus care when my way is dark
With a nameless dread and fear?
As the daylight fades
Into the deep night shades,
Does He care enough to be near?

3. Does Jesus care when I've tried and failed,
To resist some temptation strong;
When in my deep grief, I find no relief,
Tho' my tears flow all the night long?

Chorus O, yes He cares; I know He cares;
His heart is touched with my grief;
When the days are weary, the long nights dreary,
I know my Saviour cares…
(By Frank E. Graeff 1860-1919)

There is no problem too difficult for God to handle. Put your problems in the 'things to do' box and do not take them out again. We are so much in the habit of praying about our problems and worrying sick about them, as though God is not capable of dealing with them, or He is taking too long, but God's timing is different from ours; His ways are past finding out and they are higher than our ways. The prayer of relinquishment is in giving the situation to God, taking your hands off it completely, and trusting the 'One' who is qualified to handle the problem ***'And we know that all things that happen to us are working for our good if we love God and are fitting into His plans'*** (Romans 8:28 TLB). Prayer is the communication link that causes us not to worry but to trust in an all-wise God who knows what He is doing. So you are not to struggle with the situation but to commit it to God and have a peace about it.

Don't be afraid to come to God through His son Jesus Christ through the power of the Holy Spirit. The writer of Hebrews says:

'But Jesus the Son of God is our great High Priest… who has gone to heaven … to help us; therefore let us never stop trusting him. This high priest of ours understands our weakness, since he had the same temptations we do, though he never once gave way to them and sinned. So let us come boldly to the very throne of God and stay there to receive His mercy and to find grace to help us in our times of need' (Hebrews 4:14-16 TLB).

The one who sits on this throne is the Sovereign Ruler of the universe. He is also our Abba Father, 'Our Papa'; He calls us sons and daughters, so get acquainted and connected. He gives us benefits that we cannot give ourselves. Jesus says, ***"…You can ask Him for anything, using my name, and I will do it, for this will bring praise to the Father because of what I, the Son, will do for you. Yes ask anything, using my name, and I will do it!"*** (John 14:13-14 TLB). Yes He gives us what we don't deserve and could never earn, that is, His unmerited favour, from a throne room that never runs low on its provision and supplies and it is all tied to our drawing near to God in prayer. We can 'draw near with confidence to the throne of grace…' We don't have to be ashamed and hold back anything in our prayer or don't have to wonder if we are wasting our time.

God has all the grace we need to help us, but we have to go before His throne to ask for it. The prayer-less Christian however, is also a grace-less and power-less Christian. Christians who are not making prayer a way of life, are not growing in their spiritual capacity because they are not connected to the throne that dispenses grace graciously. The grace we receive at God's throne is designed to help us 'in time of need', think about that. Grace is given based on the need at a particular time whenever necessary. God will not give you tomorrow's grace until tomorrow. He gives us our daily bread each day. That is why it is important to make your supplication each day, to receive your provision of grace through Jesus Christ. So you cannot go to God too often! Prayer gives God the authority to act in the earth realm and in the realm of the spirit on man's behalf.

God is our good Shepherd and we will not have need for anything. He lets us rest in the meadow with pastures that are green and leads us beside the quiet streams. He restores our failing health. He helps us do what honours him the most. Our God provides delicious food in the presence of our enemies. He welcomes us as His guest with blessings overflowing! His goodness shall be with us all of our lives, and afterwards we will live with Him forever in His home (Psalm 23 TLB).

Do you feel as though you are in a tunnel and you cannot see the light at the end? Don't turn back because Jesus is about to turn on the light, He is the light of the world. As a matter of fact, you are poised for a miracle. He promised not to deny you, ***'For Jehovah God is our Light and our Protector. He gives us grace and glory. No good thing will He withhold from those who walk along His paths'*** (Psalm 84:11TLB). We just need to tap into His resources by praying because it activates the promises of God.

One vivid example recorded in the Book of 1Samuel 1 and 2 (TLB) is the story of a praying barren woman Hannah. Elkanah had two wives, Hannah who did not bear children and Peninnah, who had some children. They would go to the temple Shiloh yearly to worship and to sacrifice unto the Lord. Elkanah would give Peninnah and her children presents for celebrations and although he loved Hannah very much, he would give her only one present. The Lord had sealed up her womb for His purpose. Peninnah used the opportunity to harass Hannah by scoffing and laughing at her, to make her fret, especially each year as they travelled up to Shiloh, so she wept and did not eat. Elkanah would say to her "What's the matter…Why make such a fuss over having no children? Isn't having me better than having ten sons?"

Once when they had eaten and drunk in Shiloh, Eli the priest observed Hannah as he sat upon a seat by a post of the temple of the Lord. She was in bitterness of soul and prayed unto the Lord and wept sorely. She then made a vow to God, saying, "O Lord of heaven, if you will look down upon my sorrow and answer my prayer and give me a son, then I will give him back to you, and he'll be yours for his entire lifetime, and his hair shall never be cut." There are times when God would push us to the limit, which would cause us to make a vow or a commitment to Him. This vow though, must be lined up with His will, which confers with the leading of the Holy Spirit and must be kept.

As Hannah spoke Eli marked her mouth moving as she prayed silently and, hearing no sound, he thought she had been drinking. He retorted "Must you come here drunk? Throw away your bottle." She replied "O, no Sir! I am not drunk! But I am sad and I was pouring out my heart to the Lord. Please don't think that I am just some drunken bum!" Eli's response was "In that case, cheer up! May the Lord of Israel grant you your petition, whatever it is!" (1Samuel 1:14-16 TLB).

The entire family was up early the next morning and went to the Tabernacle to worship the Lord once more. Then they returned home to Ramah, and when Elkanah slept with Hannah, the Lord remembered her petition. In the process of time, a baby boy was born to her. She named him Samuel, meaning, 'Asked of God', because, as she said, "I asked the Lord for him." She did not go up to Shiloh the next year. She said "I will wait until the baby is weaned, and then I will take him to the Tabernacle and leave him there." So she stayed at home until the baby was weaned.

When he was weaned although he was still so small, they took him to the Tabernacle in Shiloh, along with a three year old bullock and one bushel of flour, and a bottle of wine. After the sacrifice they took the child to Eli. She said "Sir, do you remember me? I am the woman who stood here that time praying to the Lord! I asked him to give me this child, and he has given me my request; and now I am giving him to the Lord for as long as he lives." She kept her promise and left him there at the Tabernacle for the Lord's purpose. Hannah's prayer is more of a thanks-giving and praise. This is in effect what she said:

"How I rejoice in the Lord! How he has blessed me! Now I have an answer for my enemies, for the Lord has solved my problem. How I rejoice! No one is as holy as the Lord! There is no other God. Nor any Rock like our God. Quit acting so proud and arrogant! ...Those who were mighty are mighty no more! Those who were well are now starving; those who were starving are fed. The barren woman now has seven children; she with many children has no more! The Lord gives life ...He cuts one down and lifts another up. He lifts the poor from the dust – Yes, from a pile of ashes-and treats them as princes; sitting in the seats of honour. For all the earth is the Lord's and He sets the world in order. ...No one shall succeed by

strength alone … he judges throughout the earth… and gives great glory to his anointed one" (1Samuel 2: 1-10).

God favoured Hannah by allowing her to give birth to the prophet Samuel. He caused her to be barren and to be aggravated by Peninnah, making her desperate to have a child. After trying for years to have a child and did not succeed, she knew the next best thing was to take the matter to God, who is able to make the impossible possible. God set up the whole matter because He knew that Eli was getting old and he would soon need a priest to replace him at Shiloh. God also knew that Hannah was worthy to have such a blessing from Him. Travailing prayers end barrenness; birth prophetic movements in the correct times and seasons; open the windows of heaven; silence the enemy (adversary) and activate praise and worship to God.

What is the barren situation in your life at present? That dry parched arid desert area where you are, you feel as though you cannot take it any more. You are being **persecuted, pursued, pressured, presumed** wrongly, **pressed** to the limit, **pushed** around. Don't lose hope: you are **positioned** and **poised** for a miracle, but God would not just drop it in your lap, you have to tarry and travail for it. Pray until something happens. Many people would not understand your situation, Eli did not understand Hannah; as a matter of fact he did not even have the spirit of discernment to detect a drunken woman from a burdened woman. The Bible says the **prayer** of a righteous man or woman avails much.

The crisis you are facing today could be the beginning of a new adventurous life for tomorrow, it can be a blessing in disguise, an opportunity for greatness, greater dimensions of God's power in your life, an avenue to your ministry and the upward climb of a mountain top experience. **Persevere** and **prevail** in **prayer,** even though you do not feel like it, do it, you will be glad you did. There are times when we are so depressed that all we feel like doing is brood in the situation or want to give up. We may not be understood by our friends, family, husband, wife, or a Pastor, as it is often said 'Only who feels it knows it'. God understands and He is touched with the feelings of our infirmity. Keep the dream alive. Just as Hannah was **persuaded** in her mind that she needed to **pray** and fast, you also can **pursue** and reach your goal and ambitions in life by these **positive** measures, so that you can receive your **promotion** or a new **position**.

Fight the forces of hell, for your destiny and purpose, down on your knees. ***'For our weapons are not carnal, but mighty through God to the pulling down of the strong holds'*** (11Corinthians 10:4) of the enemy in your life. There are times you cannot do it on our own and you need a **prayer partner**, to stand with you and intercede with you, for your children, your neighbour, your community, your country etc. The Psalmist says ***'Hear my cry, O God; attend unto my prayer. From the end of the earth will I cry unto thee, when my heart is overwhelmed: lead me to the rock that is higher than I. For thou has been a shelter for me, and a strong tower from the enemy. I will abide in thy tabernacle forever: I will trust in the covert of thy wings'*** (Psalm 61:1-4 KJV).

Peter's Deliverance through corporate Prayer

It is recorded in Acts 12: 1-16 (TLB) that Herod had just executed James, and the Jewish leaders were so pleased they went and arrested Peter and imprisoned him, placing him under the guard of sixteen soldiers, with the intention to execute him after the Passover. Earnest prayer was going up to God from the Church for his safety all the time while he was in prison.

That night before he was to be executed, he was asleep (not awake and worrying), double-chained between two soldiers, with others standing guard before the prison gate, when suddenly there was a light in the cell and an angel of the Lord stood beside Peter. The angel slapped him on the side of his face to awake him and said, "Quick! Get up!" And the chains fell off his wrists! Then the angel told him, "Get dressed and put on your shoes." And he did. "Now put on your coat and follow me!" the angel ordered.

Peter left the cell, following the angel, but Peter thought that it was a dream or a vision, and didn't believe that it was really happening. They passed the first and second cell blocks and came to the iron gates to the street, and this opened to them of its own accord! So they passed through and walked along together for a block, and then the angel left him.

Finally Peter realized what had happened! "It's really true!" he said to himself. "The Lord has sent his angel and saved me from Herod and from what the Jews were hoping to do to me!" He went to the door of Mary, mother of John Mark, where many were gathered for a prayer meeting. He knocked at the door in the gate, and a girl named Rhoda came to open it. When she recognized Peter's voice, she was so overjoyed that she ran back inside to tell everyone that Peter was standing outside in the street. They didn't believe her…meanwhile Peter continued knocking. When they finally went out and opened the door, their surprise knew no bounds, they could not believe their eyes.

If you feel your prayers alone aren't getting the job done, get help, bring in reinforcement. The Bible says one shall chase a thousand but two shall put ten thousand to flight. Jesus said, ***'If two of you…agree about anything that they shall ask, it shall be done for them of my Father which is in heaven'*** (Matthew 18:19). Just come in agreement and stand on His promises and pass the situation over to Him, God is our Champion and our Great Deliverer. There are some prayers that God will answer right away, because they need urgent attention, while others take varying times to be processed, that depends on our Sovereign God, His timing is perfect. Let us come boldly one more time to the throne of grace as we pray this warfare prayer, to break dead-locked situations in our lives:

“God I come in the name of my Saviour Lord and King Jesus Christ, my Redeemer, Captain and Champion of my soul. You, Oh God are my Jehovah Shalom, the Holy One of Israel, my Rock, my Defence, my Strong and Mighty Tower, the One I serve and adore. I take authority over the forces of hell, I counter attack the forces of darkness: it is not by might, it is not by power but by the Spirit of the Living God. I break all yokes and bondages off my life by the blood of Jesus Christ, by the power of the Holy Ghost and by the authority invested within me. The gates of hell shall not prevail against the plan and purpose of God in my life.

I tread upon principalities, powers and rulers of darkness in wicked and high places which would try to oppose or hinder the original purpose, plans, dreams, goals, ambitions in my life. God has not given me a Spirit of fear but of power, love and of a sound mind. I decree that any bondage, wicked designs, connections and links are broken now. I forbid and disallow, dismantle any diabolical discussions, decisions, assignments and sanctions over my life, which may try to undermine my positions, the ones God has ear-marked for me. I am not afraid of any terror by night or any arrow that flies at noon-day because God has blessed me and I am seated in Heavenly places with Christ Jesus. So I bind all satanic efforts and attacks and I loose their effects on my life and that of my family in the name of Jesus Christ, through the power of the Holy Spirit. I thank you Lord for answering my prayer in Jesus’ name. Amen.

Chapter 4

Sing & Dance O Barren Woman

"Sing O barren woman, you who never bore a child, burst into singing, shout for joy, you who were never in labour; because more are the children of the desolate woman than of her who has a husband" Isaiah 54: 1

You may think that God has forgotten you, because you have been termed barren spiritually or physically (cannot produce or come forth). There are women in all types of situations, those who are engaged in promiscuous relationships, those who have been molested at a tender age, and others whose lives are not 'straight' like living a lesbian lifestyle or hooked on drugs. They may have children who are not doing well in school; they may be also hooked on drugs or have become rebellious for some reason or another; those who do not have the fathers to take care of their children. Many of these women are also experiencing financial disasters. God is saying to you today that all is not lost, there is hope for you. Although you find yourself in difficult straits of life, don't give up.

Your situation could be like the woman who came to the well to draw water late in the evening when all the other women of the village would have drawn their water earlier in the day. Jesus went straight to the heart of the problem. He said to her "Go…get your husband"… "I don't have one" she replied. Jesus said "You are right, you have had five husbands, and you aren't married to the man you're living with" (John 4: 16-18 NLT).

She perceived that He was a prophet so she left her water-pot and went into the village and said, "Come see a man, who told me all that I have done, the one they call Christ" He was different from all the men she had met. When we are weak we keep getting into situations that leave us wounded, and those wounds cannot be healed by going from one relationship to another; her answer was in meeting The Man, Jesus Christ, and asking Him to fill the void in her life.

Regardless of how disastrous the situation is, Jesus can fix it. Barrenness in this context, does not mean that a child cannot be produced; it means that your life is not going in the right way, be it financially, spiritually, academically or otherwise. You may have lost your business; your marriage is not working. There may be problems in your life that have persisted for years and they seem to have become chronic and there is no way out and you are about to give up, it has just been too much for too long.

The bills have been piling up; the needs are just too huge. You are saying "I have been used, misused and abused, ridiculed, written off, tried, tested, tempted and rejected in all areas of my life, I cannot take it any more. There is nothing new that can happen to me, I have gone through them all, I have hit rock bottom. Yes, the bottom line is that I have failed God so many times, I don't think He will bother with me at this stage of my life, it is too late." There is hope. You need to hear this Daughter of Zion:

"Fear not, you will no longer live in shame. The shame of your youth and the sorrows of widowhood will be remembered no more, for your Creator will be your husband. The Lord of Hosts of his name; he is your Redeemer the Holy One of Israel, the God of all the earth For the Lord has called you back from your grief – a young wife abandoned by her husband. For a brief moment I abandoned you. But with great compassion I will gather you. In a moment of anger I turned my face a little while; but with everlasting love I will have pity on you, says the Lord, your Redeemer." (Isaiah 54: 4-8 TLB)

God is saying, sing in the midst of your situation. You may be saying like the children of Israel, ***"How can I sing the Lord's song in a strange land"*** (Psalm 137: 4), a land where there is famine, where it is barren, parched and dry, where there is no water and nothing grows. The only thing that is flowing is my tears; they flow night and day. I wet my pillow each night with tears; there is no one to comfort me, and no one cares." God is still saying, "Sing O barren woman."

The devil can hold you in captivity and bondage to circumstances that are not God's will, and it takes the spirit of God to break the will of the enemy over your life. Spiritual songs, Psalms, worship and praise are also weapons that you can use to break deadlock situations in your life and to bring about God's divine intervention, so set up your divine appointment and "Sing O barren woman", in spite of what your so-called-friends or neighbours would say or despite what you are going through.

In II Chronicles 20, there is an interesting story, when the children of Moab and Ammon and others came to battle with Jehoshaphat. The Bible says Jehoshaphat feared and set himself to seek the Lord and proclaimed a fast throughout all Judah. In his prayer he said to God, "We have no way to protect ourselves against this mighty army. We don't know what to do, but we are looking to you," or in other words "Our eyes are on you," (II Chronicles 20:12).

There came a word from the Lord through Jahaziel, the son of Zechariah, 'Listen King Jehoshaphat and all who live in Judah and Jerusalem! This is what the Lord says to you: "***Do not be afraid or discouraged because of this vast army, for the battle is not yours, but God's. You will not have to fight this battle. Take up your positions, stand firm and see the deliverance the Lord will give you… Do not be afraid; do not be discouraged. Go out to face them tomorrow, and the Lord will be with you"***' (II Chronicles 20: 15-17 NIV).

Jehoshaphat bowed his face to the ground and all the people fell down in worship before the Lord. Can you trust God in the midst of your own adversity and trouble to bow down with your face to the ground and worship? Early the next morning he said ***"Listen to me Judah and Jerusalem! Have faith in the Lord your God and you will be upheld; have faith in the prophets and you will be successful."*** He then appointed men to sing to the Lord and to praise him for the splendour of His holiness as they went out at the head of the army saying, **"*Give thanks to the Lord, for His love endures forever*"**(II Chronicles 20: 21 NIV).

As they began to sing and praise, the Lord set ambushes against the men of Ammon and Moab and Mount Seir who were invading Judah and they were defeated. The men of Ammon and Moab rose up against the men from Mount Seir to destroy and annihilate them. After they were finished slaughtering the men from Seir, they helped to destroy one another. When the men of Judah came to the place that overlooked the desert and looked toward the vast army, they saw only dead bodies lying on the ground, no one had escaped. So Jehoshaphat and his men went to carry off their plunder. There was so much that it took them three days to collect them. They returned to Jerusalem to the temple of the Lord with harps, lutes and trumpets. The fear of the Lord came upon all the other countries when they heard of the victory.

We need to learn to take God at His word, to trust him and stop doubting and fearing and stop taking things into our own hands, even to have our own revenge. God is able to fight our battles, just leave it to Him. Sing O barren woman and woman out of wed-lock, even though the hurt is deep, let your body be the symphony of praise and your mouth harmonize with the songs of Zion and rivers of living waters springing forth from your inner being. You can change your atmosphere, countenance, decisions, steps, motives and moods etc., just sing.

You may be down and think that God has forgotten and forsaken you but he hasn't, He will take care of you and will come through for you. He knows that you are hurting and he feels the pain that you are experiencing, He will find a way to fix it for you, so sing barren woman. He is still God and He will not change and He will do it again for you.

The Psalmist says ***"O sing unto the Lord a new song: sing unto the Lord, all the earth. Sing unto the Lord, bless his name, show forth His salvation from day to day. Declare His glory among the heathen, His wonders among all people. For the Lord is great and greatly to be praised: He is to be feared above all gods…Honour and majesty are before Him, strength and beauty are in His sanctuary"*** (Psalm 96: 1-7 KJV).

David knew how to praise and worship God; he played skillfully on his harp and composed Psalms while he was shepherding his sheep. David used to play his harp for Saul whenever an evil spirit would come upon him. Then he spent a long time in caves and dens hiding from Saul. He was close to death many times but the Lord protected him because He had a purpose for David's life; he was to be the next king of Israel. David sang a song to the Lord after God rescued him from Saul and from all his other enemies:

"Jehovah is my rock, my fortress and my Saviour. I will hide in God, who is my rock and my refuge. He is my shield and my salvation, my refuge and high tower. Thank you, O my Saviour for saving me from all my enemies. I will call upon the Lord, who is worthy to be praised. The waves of death surrounded me; floods of evil burst upon me; I was trapped and bound by hell and death; but I called upon the Lord in my distress, and He heard me from His temple. My cry reached his ears, then the earth shook and trembled; the foundations of the heavens quaked because of his wrath… He bent the heavens down and came to earth…No wonder I give thanks to you, and praises to Him - the Rock of my salvation…" (II Samuel 22).

Do you want a release from your dead-locked situations? You need to dance like David. It is recorded in II Samuel 6. David went with the people, about thirty thousand men, to bring back the Ark of God. They set the Ark of God upon a new cart and brought it out of the house of Abinadab that was on Gibeah. Uzzah and Ahio, his sons drove the new cart with David following and other leaders of Israel, who were joyously waving branches of juniper trees and playing every type of musical instrument before the Lord, such as lyres, harps, tambourines, castanets and cymbals. When they arrived at the threshing floor of Nacon, the oxen stumbled and Uzzah put out his hand to steady the Ark. Then the anger of the Lord was flared against Uzzah and he killed him for doing this, so he died there beside the Ark.

David was afraid of the Lord and asked "How can I bring the Ark home?" He took it to the home of Obededom, where it remained for three months and Obededom prospered while it was there. David heard this and decided to bring the Ark to the City of David with great celebration. After they had gone six paces, David danced before the Lord with all his might, wearing priestly clothing. Israel brought the Ark of the Lord with much shouting and blowing of trumpets. As the procession came into the city Michal, Saul's daughter (David's wife), watched from a window and saw King David leaping and dancing before the Lord and she was filled with contempt for him.

The Ark was placed inside the tent which David had prepared for it and he sacrificed burnt offerings to the Lord. Then he blessed the people and gave them presents. Michal came out to meet him and exclaimed in disgust, "How glorious the King of Israel looked today! He exposed himself to the girls along the street like a common pervert!" David retorted, "I was dancing before the Lord who chose me above your father and his family, who appointed me as leader of Israel, the people of the Lord! So I am willing to act like a fool in order to show my joy in the Lord. Yes I am willing to look even more foolish than this, but I will be respected by the girls of whom you spoke!"(II Samuel 6:22).

Michal thought that David, being a King, should not bring himself down by taking off his kingly robe and wear this priestly robe (which symbolized his role as a Priest) and expose himself before the people (in her terms). Michal's heart was so filled with pride that she felt too stuck up to sing and dance the songs of Zion. God chose to strike her with barrenness. She did not produce an off-spring for David, which showed God's displeasure at the rebuke of dancing, praise and worship. So put your dancing boots on, and your garments of praise, for a spirit of heaviness, and dance and magnify the Lord, the God of your salvation.

Your tough times may have plunged you into a depression so deep that there is nothing any one can say to you can move you out. Or you may be in a state of denial, complacency, or just don't care what happens next. Life was just too unfair? Don't develop a bad attitude to make you pine away, dry up, or allow grief to take you under and eventually die. Do not regard God's correction as rejection, see it as proof and testimony that you are His child and that He has great plans for you, so rise to the occasion and move to another level in Jesus Christ. Do not remain in your barren state; for God is about to break your barrenness and bring you into a place of productivity and prosperity.

Praise God who is the rock of your salvation, your shield and your strong tower; dance before your Lord for His mercy endures forever; His grace is sufficient for you; you are alive today because His grace has kept you, you are down on the ground, but His grace can lift you up. You could have let go and given up, residing in a mental institution but His grace and mercy kept you. ***'Let us sing unto the Lord: let us make a joyful noise to the rock of our salvation. Let us come before His presence with thanksgiving, sing psalms and spiritual songs. For the Lord is a great God, and a great King above all gods'*** (Psalm 95: 1-3KJV). He did not bring you this far to leave you; God is on your side, be happy, kind and compassionate, shine like a beacon, rejoice, for there is a new day that is about to dawn upon you.

The Lord would use you when you sing and dance in the midst of your trial and testing, even after the enemy has whipped you and you are in pain, just sing and praise God and He will use you in this time of trial to win some souls to Christ and to turn your situation around for His honour and glory. Someone is going to wonder, 'How can she sing in the midst of this crisis, something is different about her.' Whatever you go through, do not hold grudges, malice and hatred in your heart. Pray and sing to the Lord so that you can have the breakthrough and a wonderful testimony.

This is one of my favourite choruses:

Sing praises unto God sing praises (Repeat)
Hallelujah,
Sing praises unto God sing praises (Repeat)
Hallelujah,

Chorus:
For God is our King over all the earth,
Sing praises unto Him with understanding
So clap your hands and shout all ye people
For He is to be praised, to be praised.

When there's trouble in your life sing praises (Repeat)
Hallelujah,
When there's trouble in your life sing praises (Repeat)
Hallelujah
(Author unknown)

In Genesis 33, we have a situation which occurred; one so heart-rending and sad. Jacob and his household went as far as Succoth after they left Laban. There he built himself a camp, with pens for his flocks and herds. Then they arrived safely at Shechem in Canaan, and camped outside the city. He bought the land he camped on from the family of Hamor, for 100 pieces of silver.

One day Dinah, Leah's daughter went out to visit some of the neighbourhood girls, but when Shechem, son of king, Hamor the Hivite saw her, he took her and raped her. He fell deeply in love with her and tried to win her affection. He afterwards spoke to his father about it. "Get this girl for me," he demanded, "I want to marry her."

Word soon reached Jacob of what had happened, but his sons were out in the fields herding cattle, so he did nothing until their return. Meanwhile King Hamor, Shechem's father, went to talk with Jacob, arriving just as Jacob's sons came in from the fields. Jacob's sons were too shocked and angry to overlook the insult, for it was an outrage against all of them.

Hamor told Jacob, "My son Shechem is truly in love with your daughter, and longs for her to be his wife. Moreover, we invite you folks to live here among us and to let your daughters marry our sons, and we will give our daughters as wives for your young men. And you shall live among us wherever you wish and carry on your business among us and become rich!"

Then Shechem addressed Dinah's father and brothers. "Please be kind to me and let me have her as my wife," he begged. "I will give whatever you require. No matter what dowry or gift you demand, I will pay it – only give me the girl as my wife."

Her brothers then lied to Shechem and Hamor, acting dishonourably because of what Shechem had done to their sister. They said, "We couldn't possibly, for you are not circumcised. It would be a disgrace for her to marry such a man".

Dinah's brothers decided to strike a bargain with them. "I'll tell you what we'll do, if all the men will be circumcised, then we will inter marry with you and live here and unite with you to become one people. Otherwise we will take her and be on our way."

Hamor and Shechem gladly agreed and lost no time in acting upon this request, for Shechem was very much in love with Dinah and he felt that he could surely sell the idea to the other men of the city. This meant that he would do anything just to have Dinah and he was highly respected and very popular. Hamor and Shechem appeared before the city council and presented their request.

"These men are our friends," they said. "Let's invite them to live here among us and ply their trade. For the land is large enough to hold them, and we can inter-marry with them, but they will only consider staying here on one condition; that every one of us men be circumcised, the same as they are. But if we do this, then all they have will become ours and the land will be enriched. Come on; let us agree to this so they will settle among us."

The men agreed, and all were circumcised but three days later, when their wounds were sore and sensitive to every move they made, two of Dinah's brothers, Simeon and Levi took their swords, entered the city without opposition and slaughtered every man there, including Hamor and Shechem (there seemed to be no sign of resistance or fight back). They rescued Dinah from Shechem's house and returned to their camp again. Then all of Jacob's sons went over and plundered the city because their sister had been dishonoured there.

They confiscated all the flocks and herds and donkeys; everything they could lay their hands on both inside the city and outside in the fields, and took all the women and children and wealth of every kind. Then Jacob said to Levi and Simeon, "You have made me ashamed among all the people of this land; all the Canaanites and Perizzites. We are so few that they will come and crush us and we will all be killed." They retorted "Should he treat our sister like a prostitute?"

When we read this story, I think we would all wish we could rewrite it. I would write: 'as Hanor and Shechem and the men of the city were circumcised, Shechem and Dinah were married, she later became queen and Shechem was king, and had many children, and Jacob's son and his servants and the people of the city were inter-married and they also traded, everyone sticking to their agreement.

The bottom line is that Shechem was wrong to rape Dinah, but what about the reconciliation plan that was put in place of being circumcised (which they did) so that they could be covenanted like Jacob and his sons? What happened to the amendments the father and the people of the city were willing to make, where they could trade etc? Where is the spirit of forgiveness? Why did Jacob's sons have to take revenge? Why could they not put the matter in God's hand and let him fix it instead of them making such a bloody mess of things? God said 'Do not take revenge, my friends, but leave room for God's wrath, for it is written: "It is mine to avenge; I will repay," says the Lord (Romans 12: 19 NIV).

Maybe Dinah had started to have a vision of her wildest dream, that one day she would be a queen, she probably saw herself sitting at the king's table many times as she spent days in the house of Shechem. Dinah who had witnessed so much family drama, marrying a prince could have been ideal especially because of the love that Shechem expressed for her, his family had accepted her already. Her dreams were shattered and no one had even stopped to ask her opinion, she thought they had her interest at heart but it was their own agenda they were focusing on, plus they made all the decisions. There are some opportunities that knock only once and this was Dinah's once in a life time. The question is, where did Dinah go after this incident, did she go into a state of oblivion? There is no mention of Dinah in the Bible after this incident.

There are other stories of so many of our women today who are victims of abuse: verbal, physical and sexual abuse. There are many we will never hear about, they are too private and sensitive to be mentioned. There are records of rapes, incest and violence meted out to children and women in different societies of the world because they are vulnerable and helpless. There are children who are raped and killed by men who do not have hearts, some of these children who survive never live normal lives, and they were targeted to fulfill the sexual drives and satanic desires of wicked men.

We may ask when all this brutality will come to an end. What can we do that can make a difference? You may be saying when we look in the world with all this evil there is really nothing to sing and dance about. Do not lose hope for these 'barren woman'. Pray for God to change the situation in our world He can do it, we cannot go on a rampage like Simeon and Levi. Let us assist in what ever way we can to make a difference in these hurting people's lives.

'When they walk through the Valley of Weeping (Baca) it will become a place of springs where pools of blessing and refreshment collect after rains! (You)They will grow constantly in strength and each of them is (you are) invited to meet with the Lord in Zion' (Psalm 84: 6, 7 TLB).

You walk through this valley of weeping each day; you wish things can be different for you. There are times when we would want to ask God why is He permitting what is happening. You wish it did not happen or wish the hurt would go away. When it does not stop, you plunge into depression; you become discouraged, withdrawn, silent, and indifferent or wish to die. God, however, is Sovereign and the quicker you accept His terms the better it is for you.

You are finding it difficult to trust again and face life in a new dimension, but thank God for He is a Healer of broken relationships and violated trust. God is ready to heal your heart but you have to release the person who has hurt you, if even you have cause to mention it, let it be a testimony. The one who did the hurting and caused the pain may feel comfortable and happy to move on with their life without feeling guilty, but you may still feel the pain. Release them and let them go, so that you can be released from the emotional and physical pressure on your life. God can give you a new beginning, so make that decision today.

Jesus said it, ***"It's not my will, but thy will be done."*** a marriage on the rocks, a fiancé relationship that has gone sour, a once trusted business partnership in jeopardy etc. When you turn to God, He will give you the grace to endure it, embrace it, grieve, express it, release it, and go on to becoming stronger. When you come to grips with the enormity of your loss or the injustice done to you, you should be ready to forgive, but the human side of us finds it difficult. You just need to have an encounter with the Lord in Zion, the sympathizing Jesus; He understands more than we think, and He knows all about it.

You might have been molested like Dinah, it may have been some time now but you still find it hard to deal with. Give it up, don't hold on to it any longer, it is suffocating you and killing you slowly. You may have had issues in your family, where family members treated you unfairly, used or abused you, leaving you fragile and limp. Every time you remember the anger and the hurt is still there and you are finding it difficult to forgive, but forgive for Jesus' sake. Tear up the scoring cards, you do not need those records any more, the memory of them is too painful, give it all to Jesus.

You may have been fired from your job unfairly and you are holding it against your boss or supervisor but you need to release them. You may have become a mother in your early teens and it was an unwanted pregnancy. You were not able to have the formal education you dreamed of. Each time you see the child or children there is a rage that rises up within you, and now you have become abusive. Think again, do not make the vicious cycle continue with your children; forgive the father and start loving your child or children. You cannot alter the past but you can change the present.

God can cause you to have a new chapter in your story; He is not finished with you as yet. He can cause you to blossom and flourish once again. However there are some prerequisites to this requirement. God wants you to forgive, so that you can move on with your life. ***'Instead, be kind to each other, tenderhearted, forgiving one another, just as God has forgiven you because you belong to Christ'*** (Ephesians 4:32 TLB). Things may have gone wrong but God is able to turn them around. You may be hurting now but give God a chance to heal those hurts. Don't try to deal with them yourself. He can turn your battered, bruised, rejected and dejected body into His earthen vessel and your mind into the mind of Christ. 'Let this mind be in you which was in Jesus Christ' (Philippians 2:5 KJV) and your lips into a symphony of praise.

Your next level of progression for your life is for you to forgive yourself or stop blaming yourself. Dinah probably blamed herself a thousand times for going for the walk on that day. She might have thought, if I had not gone all these things would not have happened. You have the scripture, it says '***No, dear brothers, I am still not all I should be but I am bringing all my energies to bear on this one thing: Forgetting the past and looking forward to what lies ahead…'*** (Philippians 3:13TLB). Maybe for all these years you may have been saying "If only I had done it this way", you need to get out of the 'If only I' mode and move on to 'If only you can see me now, you'll be shocked.' You have been in a parked position too long, put yourself into first gear, get off the run-way, then move into second gear, keep on accelerating, change into third, because God has turned on the green light that gives you the right away to "Go". He is saying the road in front of you is clear, you can now move into fourth gear, go on now, and enjoy the ride to a new life with the Lord in Zion.

God is saying ***'I, yes, I alone am He who blots away your sins for my own sake and will never think of them again'*** (Isaiah 43:25). When God says He forgives, He forgives. He casts your sins into the sea of forgetfulness, never to remember them again. If God has forgiven you, you need to forgive those who wrongly or despitefully used you.

This takes us back to Isaiah 54: 1-8 TLB:

'Sing, O childless woman! Break out into loud and joyful song, Jerusalem, for she who was abandoned has more blessings

now than she whose husband stayed! (Despite what you went through) ***Enlarge your house; build an addition; spread out your home! For you will soon be bursting at the seams! … Fear not; you will no longer live in shame. The shame of your youth and the sorrows of widowhood will be remembered no more, for your creator will be your 'husband.' The Lord of Hosts is His name; he is your Redeemer, the Holy One of Israel, God of all the earth. For the Lord has called you back from your grief- a young wife abandoned by her husband. For a brief moment of anger I turned my face a little while; but with everlasting love I will have pity on you, says the Lord, your Redeemer'.***

You may feel as though God has forsaken you. He may have turned His face away from you for a while or He went silent, but things have just changed for the better. Please, do not be jealous of anyone, whether for their **position** or **possession** because your time will soon come for your **promotion**. You are about to expand your home, or reorganize yourself in areas of business and commerce, with entrepreneurial skills, your talent will explode, the best days are ahead of you because you have entrusted your future to the Divine will of the Omnipotent God. He promises ***'To appoint unto them that mourn in Zion, to give unto them beauty for ashes; joy instead of mourning; Praise instead of heaviness. For God has planted them (you) like strong and graceful oaks for His own glory'*** (Isaiah 61: 3 KJV). Your days of sorrow and mourning will be a thing of the past. God also says '***Arise and shine; for the light is come, and the glory of the Lord is risen upon thee'*** (Isaiah 60:1KJV). So woman of Zion arise and shine.

God may be speaking to you, woman of Zion, to spiritually adopt some children that you did not give birth to in the physical. There are some mothers who have given birth to their children but cannot take on the financial responsibility, or do not have the spiritual ability to bring them up in the 'fear of the Lord'. Let us not be selfish by just taking care of our own children but look out for those in our neighbourhood or community for those who are going astray. You never know, the child that the Lord will lead you to take care of may be marked by the enemy as a victim of gang related crimes, so save a life. God would reward you and bless you for taking on the extra responsibility. When you cast your 'bread' upon the water, by the time it comes back to you it would be swollen by so many times the original size. Adopt them, empower them, love them, clothe them, help to educate them, and snatch them from the clutches of the enemy. Don't stop to think if they would be grateful or not later on in life, God will reward you.

Declare and Decree the Word

You need to start declaring and decreeing some positive things in your life by personalizing this scripture and giving back God His word, He said He had spoken it so He is able to bring it to pass. '***O my afflicted people, tempest-tossed and troubled, I will rebuild you on a foundation of sapphires and make the walls of your houses from precious jewels. I will make your towers of sparkling agate, and your gates and walls of shining gems.***

All your children and citizens shall be taught by me, and their prosperity shall be great. You will live under a government that is just and fair. Your enemies will stay far away; you will live in peace. Terror will not come near.

I have created the blacksmith who blows the coals beneath the forge and makes the weapons of destruction. I have also created the armies that destroy and make havoc. But in that coming day, no weapon turned against you shall succeed, and

you will have justice against every courtroom lie. This is the heritage of the servants of the Lord. This is the blessing and the vindication I have given you, says the Lord' (Isaiah 54: 11-17 TLB).

You will not go through stuff in life that God has set up, and come back out with nothing, as long as you commit your way to Him. Your home probably was once a happy one with a joyful family with realistic expectations, but infidelity and broken promises came into play; destroying the dreams of life-long trust and confidence. Or you may be longing for your husband or wife to return home. In the Garden of Eden God told Eve, "…in pain you shall bring forth children…" but He did not leave it there, He went on to say, "…yet your desire shall be for your husband…"

God has promised to restore the relationship between the man and the woman and its return would be signified by a rekindled desire. That is because He knows that there's no cure for the past pain but to have a new present desire, in other words when the longing for something is powerful enough, it can wipe out the pain of the past. This helps to rekindle the fire as the Lord blows the Holy Ghost upon the relationship and the wounded and weary rise again with renewed energy and purpose.

Do you want God to fulfill His purpose in your life after all that you went through? Say this prayer with me:

Dear God through Jesus Christ and the Holy Spirit, I forgive the person/persons who have wounded me. Heal my wounded, broken spirit, forgive my sins and cleanse me of the thoughts of the past. I know that you love me and want to save me through the blood of Jesus Christ, and I thank you for that relationship. I am ready to move on with my life with you. It is not possible to do it without you holding my hand; teach me and guide me, I pray. Give me renewed strength and courage to face the world with all its ills as I step out with bold faith. You are God in Zion;

for the joy of the Lord is my strength. So I will sing and dance and rejoice in your presence for all that you have done for me, in Jesus' name, Amen.

Chapter 5

PROPHESIES, DREAMS AND VISIONS

We are living in times of hard economic crisis in our world today, in which the governments of the nations have to try and find ways and means to resolve financial problems. There are banks and institutions that have been doing fore-closures on house and vehicle owners who cannot meet their financial indebtedness. Students are finding it difficult to meet the payments to their educational institutions. Factories and manufacturers are closing down and people lose their jobs daily.

Lately there have been experiences of drastic changes in weather patterns; there is the fear of tornados and tsunami. Earthquakes have been frequent phenomena in different regions of the world, of which Haiti is recorded to have had the worst so far. We thank God for thousands who have come to the assistance of men, women and children in various ways and means by reaching out with helping hands to those who are in need of shelter, clothes, food, water, medical relief etc. They still need our help, as it going to take them years to rebuild their lives. Let us continue to help our fellowmen and let us not grow weary and faint in offering them our assistance.

The Word of God speaks expressly of a sequence of tough times as mentioned. 2 Timothy 3:1 (AMP), Paul in his writing to Timothy said ***'But understand this, that in the last days there will set in perilous times of great stress and trouble - hard to deal with and hard to bear'***. Daniel 11:32 says: ***'...but the people that do know their God shall be strong, and do exploits'***. The word of God is still relevant to every situation that we can ever go through, so you need to stay strong.

God is looking for a people who are resilient and willing and ready to be obedient to Him and who are prepared to follow Him every step of the way: whether it is through the dessert, upon the mountain, down the valley, through the storms of life. Even in the midst of hard times you can still have hope that blessings and prosperity will come. Have an attentive ear, to hear the prophetic word; keep your eyes open for His dreams and visualize His visions for your life. ***'Where there is no vision, the people perish'*** Proverbs 29:18. We shall prophesy, dream dreams and see visions.

Your dreams can be imagined series of events experienced in the mind while you are asleep, these can vary depending on the state of mind or the forces controlling the mind at the time. It is interesting here to note that you can have day-dreams (you are wide awake) and they can be just thoughts, images and sensations occurring in the mind, they can be pleasant and unpleasant. Having visions is taking it to a higher level, where you have the ability to see, think and plan for the future, using your imagination or wisdom, having a mental capacity of what you think your future is going to look like. You may not come up with the exact plan but you can come up with something close to it. Dreams and visions can be driven by God and are divinely ordained.

If you do not have visions then your dreams are not enough to take you where you need to go, it simply means that regardless to what happens in your life you just have to stay focused on your dreams so that the visions can be realized or materialized. Joseph kept the reflections of his dreams which occurred in his sleep, and which were designed by God; yet even though he went through hard times, he worked and focused on his visions, and although the obstacles were tough, without his visions, he would have been doomed.

The Lord who created you is saying: ***"Don't be afraid, for I have ransomed you; I have called you by name; you are mine. When you go through deep waters and great trouble, I will be with you. When you go through rivers of difficulty, you will not be burned up-the flames will not consume you. For I am the Lord your God, your Saviour, the Holy One of Israel…Others died that you might live; I traded their lives for yours because you are precious to me and honoured, and I love you."*** (Isaiah 43:1-4 TLB)

Are you ready to run with the dream and vision that God has created and crafted for you? Remember, 'He does not call the qualified but he qualifies the called'. God will place in your grasp the resources necessary to fulfill the call, be it a Politician, Church Leader, Youth Pastor or Lawyer. He will surround you with the right people and elements that will push you into your destiny and to accomplish His plan and purpose. He did not say it was going to be easy but He did say when you call He would be there, in the tough times and in the cool days.

Do you have an unthinkable, scary, drastic, absolutely wild and impossible idea that would make others' hair stand up on the top of their head, or think that you are crazy, or cause you to lose your night's sleep, or it makes you so restless that you know you can never be comfortable until you go for it? That's the way dreams are supposed to be, especially if they are of God, He has hand-picked you for this season, this era, this time, to bring forth change in your family, school, job, community, country, region or maybe to have a positive impact on the world.

'After I have poured out my rains again, I will pour out my Spirit upon all of you! Your sons and daughters will prophesy; your old men will dream dreams, your young men see visions' (Joel 2:28 TLB).

If when you are going through, you are faced with some challenges and turbulent times, know that they are training grounds for your big assignment/s. There would be obstacles such as time, finance, reasoning, geographical boundaries, family barriers, cultural differences, education, religion, the matter of the colour of your skin and being 'politically correct or incorrect' can pose problems. These may be some hurdles that are not easy to jump over and conquer but it can be accomplished by faith. It takes visionary eyes to see beyond those of your skeptics. A life is worth nothing until it is used for doing the work assigned by the Lord Jesus.

There are those people who have worked tirelessly behind the scenes in prayer, who have bruised their knees for you, speaking words of encouragement into your life and also giving moral support wherever necessary. On the other hand there were some of you who were not so fortunate but had to learn by error, had no support, had to go through some struggles, learn the hard way, being rejected, shut off, termed as drop-outs, brought up in the ghettos, misunderstood, worked hard and long hours at tough jobs, maybe two and three jobs at a time. The paradox here is: only these persons and God could see their road map clearly because they are the ones God chose to fulfill their specific calling, so let us not judge them wrongfully.

We may ask ourselves, "What is behind great accomplishments?" It is a fighting spirit, pursuit of willpower, perseverance, great people, dream makers, vision keepers. Disregard the dream-killers, stick to the plan of God. Age, gender, heritage, talent, culture or environment should not prevent you; let your faith in God push you through. He will give you the **power** to **prepare**, **perform**, **perfect** and **promote** your dreams and visions. There are numerous ordained Prophets, Dream Makers and Visionaries recorded in the Word of God. Let us look at some examples and the legacies they have left behind for us to pattern our lives from. There are many male prophets mentioned in the Bible but we just want to look at one female prophetess, not for discriminatory reasons.

Deborah the Prophetess

It is recorded in the Book of Judges Chapter 4, that the children of Israel again did evil in the sight of the Lord when Ehud a deliverer, a Benjamite died. The Lord let them be conquered by King Jabin of Hazor, in Canaan. The commander-in-chief was Sisera. He had nine hundred iron chariots and made life unbearable for the Israelites for twenty years but finally they begged the Lord for help.

At this time the one who was responsible for bringing the people back to God was Deborah, a prophetess, the wife of Lappidoth. She held court at a place called 'Deborah's Palm Tree,' where the people came to settle their disputes. One day she summoned Barak, saying to him, "The Lord God of Israel has commanded you to mobilize ten thousand men from the tribes of Naphtali and Zebulun. You must lead them to Mount Tabor, to fight King Jabin's mighty army with all his chariots, under General Sisera's command. The Lord says, 'I will draw them to the Kishon River, and you will defeat them there.'" Barak told her that he would not go up unless she went with him.

She told him, "All right, I'll go with you; but I'm warning you now that the honour of conquering Sisera will go to a woman instead of you!" So she went with him to Kedesh. When Sisera was told that Barak and his army were camped at Mount Tabor, he mobilized his entire army, including the nine hundred iron chariots, and marched from Harosheth-ha-goiim to the Kishon River.

Deborah said to Barak, “Now is the time for action! The Lord leads on! He has already delivered Sisera into your hand!” Barak then led his ten thousand men down the slopes of Mount Tabor into battle. Then the Lord threw the enemy into a panic, both the soldiers and the charioteers, and Sisera leaped from his chariot and escaped on foot. Barak and his men chased the enemy and the chariots as far as Harosheth-ha-goiim, until all of Sisera’s army was destroyed; not one man was left alive.

Meanwhile, Sisera had escaped to the tent of Jael; the wife of Heber the Kenite, for there was a mutual-assistance agreement between King Jabin of Hazor and the clan of Heber. Jael went out to meet Sisera and said to him, “Come into my tent, sir. You will be safe here in our protection. Don’t be afraid.” So he went into her tent and she covered him with a blanket. “Please give me some water,” he said, “for I am very thirsty.” She gave him some milk and covered him again.

“Stand in the door of the tent,” he told her, “and if anyone comes by looking for me, let them know that no one is here.” Then Jael took a sharp tent peg and a hammer and quietly creeping up to him as he slept, she drove the peg through his temples and into the ground; and so he died, for he was fast asleep from weariness.

When Barak came by looking for Sisera, Jael went out to meet him and said, “Come and I will show you the man you are looking for.” He followed her into the tent and found Sisera lying there dead, with the tent peg through his temples. That day the Lord used Israel to subdue King Jabin of Canaan. From that time on Israel became stronger and stronger against King Jabin, until he and all his people were destroyed. After that Deborah and Barak sang a song about the wonderful victory and peace was in the land forty years.

This was a time of victory for the children of Israel through the valiant work and prophetic word of the prophetess Deborah. The Bible records few women in national leadership positions, but Deborah was obviously the best person for the job, and God used her to lead Israel in her time. God does not take sides, neither is He a gender-biased God. He can choose anyone to lead His people, young or old, man or woman. Do not let your prejudices get in the way of those God may have chosen to lead you.

We are not certain if Barak was a coward or if he just needed support but we have seen the character of a great leader and a judge in Deborah, who took charge as God directed. Deborah told Barak that God would be with him in battle, but that was not enough for him. Barak wanted Deborah to go with him; this request shows that at heart he trusted human strength more than God's promise. A person of real faith steps out at God's command, even if he or she must do so alone.

Deborah commanded Israel's respect and also that of Barak, a military general. She was able to influence them after the battle was over to live for God. They knew they could trust the prophetic word coming forth from her and the victory in battle attested to the fact that she was hearing from God. Also as a prophetess, her main role was to encourage the people to obey God. Those who lead must not forget about the spiritual condition of those being led. A true leader must be concerned for the welfare of persons, not just their success.

Jael must be commended for the accomplishment of her surprise attack on Sisera. Her husband Herber decided to side with Jabin, maybe because Jabin's army appeared to have the military advantage. Although Herber joined forces with Jabin, his wife did not. Sisera thought that he was in good hands when Jael offered her tent as a hiding place; he felt that no one would know that he was there. Women in that day were responsible for pitching the tents and Jael had no problem driving the tent peg into Sisera's head while he slept. Deborah's prediction was thus fulfilled: the honour of conquering Sisera went to this noble woman, Jael and the victory of the battle went to Deborah as she had said to Barak.

If God called you as a woman to lead and you are afraid because of gender issues, don't be scared because God has you covered. God says, ***'Don't be afraid…I am with you,'*** so ask yourself what He wants and stop worrying about people pleasing. Solomon said, ***'Fear of human opinion disables you'*** (Proverbs 29:25 TM). When you look back at what you've already overcome you begin to realize that most times failure doesn't do permanent damage – but it actually helps you to mature and grow during the processing period! So stay focused; with God, you can do whatever He calls you to do. Who knows, you might even begin to enjoy the challenge! So what's keeping you from asking God to allow you to get involved now before you miss out on your God given assignment? Position yourself to receive His direct intervention and directive as soon as possible.

Maybe you have not been called to lead but to be part of a team or a co-leader like Barak. God has given us the ability to do certain things well. Find out what are your greatest strengths and build on them, you will become matured and secured with time. There are times when you will feel insecure and uncomfortable when you face new issues or territories, don't let your feelings of doubt take control of you, just be flexible and adjust to change, you would grow and develop after a while. Spend some time exploring yourself, finding out what your gifts are. Ask God questions: the Holy Spirit will equip you with answers. Ask for feedback on performances, be prepared for criticisms, take responsibility but make amends.

Barak trusted Deborah, so trust your leader and support him or her. If a person finds that they can't work with their leader, let them find another leader and avoid conflict. Let the sky be your goal or limit, in other words look at the bigger picture, get out of the box and don't put yourself down even though you make mistakes. Don't just look out for yourself or personal gains but be there for others. Wrong motives would diminish your joy. Find some fulfillment in serving, it is Jesus' desire for us to serve others and in so doing you would not necessarily desire success in order to achieve, so do it out of a heart of love. Go ahead, discover your skills, take risks and good advice, make mistakes, try things, and learn from your failures and successes and love others more than your self. Discover what God has designed you for.

Joseph: the Dreamer

Let's look at the life of Joseph (as recorded in Genesis 37-45 TLB), a dreamer as he is sometimes called. At the age of seventeen Joseph had to work along with his brothers as a shepherd and Jacob loved Joseph more than all his other children. One day Jacob gave him a brightly-coloured coat and his brothers of course took notice of the particular love and consequently hatred developed.

One night Joseph had a dream and promptly reported the details to his brothers, causing even deeper hatred. "Listen to this" he said proudly, "We were out in the field binding sheaves, and my sheaf stood up, and your sheaves all gathered around it and bowed low before it."

"So you want to be our king, do you?" his brothers derided, and they hated him for the dream and for his cocky attitude. Then he had another dream and again he told it to his brothers. "Listen to my latest dream," he boasted, "The sun, moon, and eleven stars bowed low before me!" This time his father rebuked him "What is this? He asked, "Shall I indeed, and your mother and brothers come and bow before you?" His brothers envied him; but his father wondered what it meant.

Joseph's brothers were already angry over the possibility of being ruled by their little brother. Hearing of another dream fueled the fire because of his boastful attitude. We have to be careful with whom we share our dreams; it can cause hatred and malice to develop. Not every one will want us to succeed in life, and sometimes the hatred comes from our household or those closest to us.

This time Jacob sent Joseph to Shechem to look out for his brothers. He had to go on to Dothan where they were and when they saw him coming they recognized him in the distance because of the coat. They exclaimed "Here comes the dreamer, come on, let us kill him and toss him into a well and tell father that a wild animal has eaten him. Then we'll see what becomes of his dreams!"

Reuben, hoping to spare Joseph's life said "Let us not kill him, we'll shed no blood, let's throw him alive into this well here; that way he'll die without us touching him." Reuben was planning to get him out later and return him to his father. When Joseph got there they pulled off his brightly coloured robe and threw him into an empty well.

There are some people who would hate you for your dreams, even people in your family house hold and the house hold of faith. There are times when the enemy will throw you in a pit or well, you will find that you may be all alone experiencing darkness, hunger, hatred, depression and oppression but keep your dream and your vision alive because it is only for a time. Reuben means 'Surely the Lord hath looked upon my affliction', he intended to rescue Joseph and look upon his affliction but God had another plan.

Later, as they sat down to eat; suddenly they noticed a string of camels coming towards them in the distance, probably Ishmaelite traders who were taking gum, spices, and herbs from Gilead to Egypt. Judah said to the others, "Let us sell Joseph to them! Why kill him and have a guilty conscience? Let us not be responsible for his death, for after all he is our brother!" His brothers agreed so they went to the traders and pulled Joseph out and sold him for twenty pieces of silver, and he was then taken to Egypt. Reuben came later and found that he was not there; he ripped his clothes in anguish and frustration.

God will always deliver on time. It was not God's will for Joseph to die in the pit, He had other plans: this was just the beginning of a long and hard journey. ***'The exile will soon be set free, and will not die in the dungeon, nor will his bread be lacking'*** (Isaiah 51:14). God determines what our location will be, at what time, for what purpose, for how long, what qualification is necessary so that we can fit the task and position He has ordained for us.

They went to Jacob with Joseph's coat splattered with goat's blood, saying a wild animal had eaten him. There are times the people you come into contact with think that they will destroy God's plan in your life. They push you through some tough times, making sure that your life is miserable and unbearable; but it may be the very thing that is necessary to groom you for your future and the process that God will use to fashion you.

Although Joseph's brothers didn't kill him outright, they probably didn't expect him to survive for long as a slave. They were quite willing to let cruel slave traders do their dirty work for them. He faced a 30-day journey through the desert, probably chained on his feet, maybe treated like baggage, and once in Egypt, he would be sold as a piece of merchandise. His brothers thought they would never see him again but they were wrong, God was very much at work in his life.

The traders sold Joseph to Potiphar, an officer of the Pharaoh – the king of Egypt. Potiphar was also a captain of the palace guard, the chief executioner. Joseph had quite a lot to think about on his journey down to Egypt but was able to make his first cultural adjustment in the house of Potiphar. The Lord blessed him in the home of his master, so that everything he did succeeded. Potiphar realized that the Lord was with Joseph in a very special way. Joseph naturally became a favourite with him and was soon put in charge of the administration of Potiphar's household affairs.

His crops flourished and his stock multiplied. God was training and processing Joseph for things to come. He also had to show that there was a special gifting on Joseph's life so that he would move in line with what He was preparing him for. Potiphar soon gave him complete administrative responsibility over everything he owned, except his wife. Potiphar's wife observed this and one day she began making eyes at Joseph and suggested that he come and sleep with her.

Joseph refused and told her, "Look, my master trusts me with everything in the entire household! He himself has no more authority here than I have! He has held back nothing from me except you, because you are his wife. How can I do such a wicked thing as this? It will be a great sin against God."

She kept on with her suggestions day after day, even though he refused to listen, and kept out of her way as much as possible. Then one day as he was in the house going about his work, no one else was around at the time, she came and grabbed him by the sleeve demanding, "Sleep with me." He tore himself away but as he did, his jacket slipped off and she was left holding it as he fled from the house.

She saw that he had fled, so she began screaming. When the other men came running in to see what had happened, she was crying hysterically. "My husband brought this Hebrew slave to insult us, he tried to rape me, but when I screamed he ran and forgot to take his jacket!" she exclaimed. Joseph was thrown in prison where the king's prisoners were kept in chains, but the Lord was with Joseph there too, and was kind to him by granting him favour with the chief jailer. Joseph spent thirteen years in prison.

You might have been planted in a church for quite some years but there is a Mrs. Potiphar who the enemy has been using to try to get you to sin, yes it happens in the church. Their bodies should be the temple of the living God but their minds have not been renewed, so the enemy will use them to get you who are serving God faithfully, to sin. They recognize that you are strong but they want to break your will, scandalize your name and tell lies on you but be aware. Stand tall and be a Joseph, later on you will be able to look back over your life and see what the Lord delivered you from and how He brought you through.

There might be some Josephs who were once serving the Lord but because of certain situations were not able to overcome the wicked one and were enticed by the world, the flesh and the devil, God wants you to come back. Jeremiah 3: 21-22 (TLB) says: ***"I hear voices high upon the wind-swept mountains, crying, crying. It is the sons of Israel who have wandered far away. O my rebellious children come back to me again and I will heal you from your sins. And they reply, yes we will come, for you are the Lord our God."*** If you are hearing God's voice right now talking to you, do not harden your heart nor stiffen your neck, but come to Jesus in true repentance.

While in prison, Potiphar assigned Joseph to wait on the Pharaoh's chief baker and the wine taster. One night each of them had a dream, the next morning they were both sad. They told Joseph their dreams, to which Joseph gave them the correct interpretations. "Please have some pity on me when you are back in his favour, and mention me to Pharaoh, and ask him to let me out of here. For I was kidnapped from my homeland among the Hebrews and now I am in jail when I did nothing to deserve it" Joseph pleaded.

The dreams were fulfilled when three days after, it was Pharaoh's birthday, and he held a party for all of his officials and household staff. He sent for the wine taster and chief baker, and they were brought to him. He restored the wine taster to his former position but the chief baker was hanged just as Joseph had said. The wine taster promptly forgot what Joseph had requested.

One night two years later Pharaoh dreamed that he was standing on the bank of the Nile River when suddenly, seven sleek, fat cows came up out of the river and began grazing in the grass. Then seven other cows came up from the river, but they were very skinny and all their ribs stood out. They went over and stood beside the fat cows. Then the skinny cows ate the fat ones! At which point Pharaoh woke up. He had another dream which was quite similar.

Pharaoh knew the dreams were significant and needed interpretation. He called for all the magicians and sages of Egypt and told them about his dreams, but none of them could suggest what the dreams meant. Then the king's wine taster spoke up. He only at this time remembered that while he was in prison that Joseph had interpreted his and the baker's dream correctly. Pharaoh then sent for Joseph, he was brought hastily out of the dungeon, and after a quick shave and change of clothes, came in before Pharaoh.

Pharaoh told Joseph that he heard he could interpret dreams but Joseph replied, "I can't do it by myself, but God will tell you what it means." How many times, even as Christians, we forget that we cannot do anything of ourselves but it is through the power and enablement of Jesus Christ. 'I can do all things through Christ who strengthens me' (Philippians 4:13 NKJV).

Joseph said to Pharaoh "Both dreams meant the same thing. God was telling you what he is going to do here in the land of Egypt. The seven fat cows (and also the seven fat, well-formed heads of grain) mean that there are seven years of prosperity ahead. The seven skinny cows (and also the seven thin and withered heads of grain) indicate that there will be seven years of famine following the seven years of prosperity."

"God has showed you what he is about to do: The next seven years will be a period of great prosperity but afterwards there will be seven years of famine so great that all prosperity will be forgotten and wiped out; famine will consume the land. The famine will be so terrible that even the memory of the good years will be erased. The double dream gives double impact, showing that what God has told you is certainly going to happen soon. My suggestion is that you find the wisest man in Egypt and put him in charge of administering a nation-wide farm program."

"Let Pharaoh divide Egypt into five administrative districts, and let the officials of these districts gather into the royal storehouses all the excess crops of the next seven years, so that there will be enough to eat when the seven years of famine come. Otherwise disaster will surely strike."

Joseph's suggestions were well received by Pharaoh and his assistants. As they discussed who should be appointed for the job, Pharaoh said, "Who could do it better than Joseph? He is a man who is obviously filled with the Spirit of God." Turning to Joseph, Pharaoh said to him, "Since God has revealed the meaning of the dreams to you; you are the wisest in the country! I am hereby appointing you to be in charge of this entire project. What you say goes, throughout all the land of Egypt. I alone will outrank you." If God has called you to do a project or a job etc, He would endow you with the wisdom above other counterparts, so abide with what ever or where ever you are going through right now because it will qualify you for the job later.

Pharaoh placed his own signet ring on Joseph's finger as a token of his authority, and dressed him in beautiful clothing and placed the royal golden chain about his neck and declared, "See I have placed you in charge of all the land of Egypt." From out of a dungeon straight to a governor! What a promotion, only God could do that! Joseph met the criteria, passed the tests and was qualified. God's timing was perfect. I guess Joseph's spirit was daunted at times because it was such a long period and arduous journey, being innocently tossed into prison, but he never gave up.

God set up this appointment for Joseph by tossing the wine taster and the baker into the prison and they having dreams for Joseph to interpret, so as to bring Joseph before the Pharaoh himself. He was strategically and divinely placed by God all the way, even though his situations did not seem like favourable ones. He was preparing him all along for leadership. Joseph may have wondered at times if God had forgotten him in the prison. The butler and the baker forgot but God did not forget. God took him from his kindred at the right time to the right locations for the right training and fit him for the right position.

Do not disregard your connections for each location you pass through, even though it is a pit or a prison. Be sure to leave a report of good conduct; in other words, sow good seeds so that you can reap a bountiful harvest. You never know who is going to remember the little deeds of kindness, the words of comfort, encouragement, the friendship and the reaffirming of personalities that you have helped to mold or the training you have passed on. These things would work for your benefit later on the journey, as these same friends would now come back to bless you. As the word of God says ***'Cast your bread upon the water for you will find it after many days'*** (Ecclesiastes 11:1 NKJV).

The Lord was also testing Joseph's character; this also shows that the road to success is not easy. It involves having dreams that could cause people to question you or doubt your dreams, or would go all out to destroy them. You have to hold on to your dream despite the difficulties that come your way, even in the toughest and hardest of times. Folks may doubt your integrity, dignity, loyalty, credibility, honesty, even your ability to function and to be successful but hold on to your dream.

You may face temptation, frustration, you want to give up, and you may even think 'no this cannot be God; He would not let me go through this. God, how long you will you forget me, where are you, when is my dream going to be fulfilled?' Hold on, there is nothing that God brings you to, that He cannot bring you through.

'Dear brothers, is your life full of difficulties and temptations? Then be happy, for when the way is rough, your patience has a chance to grow. So let it grow, and don't squirm out of your problems. For when your patience is finally in full bloom, then you will be ready for anything, strong in character, full and complete' (James 1:2-4 TLB)

It involves being humble so that God could exalt you in due course of time. You may feel like retaliating, Jesus did not revile even though He was suffering at the hands of his torturers. It involves staying focused, so you would not lose sight of your goals, vision, dreams and ambitions. Stay positive, even around those who are despitefully using you or judging you wrongfully. It also means staying so prepared that even though your dreams are delayed, you know that God is working behind the scenes, or that He may open the door at any time, it may be when you least expect it but you are fully ready to walk through it. The Bible says '***Until the time came to fulfill his dreams the Lord tested Joseph's character'*** (Psalm 105:19 NLT). He never lost sight of his dreams.

You may wonder at times why your life is so difficult, nothing seems to work for you, you keep going through these meandering stages; they are your tests. When you are in school you are given tests to see what you have learned, in order for you to be promoted. As it is in the natural, so it is in the spiritual and supernatural. When your test comes flex your spiritual muscles, develop spine and stamina. Do not genuflect to the gods of the world, do not give in to fleshly desires; do not blow situations out of proportion. Do not bow to the devil's wishes that will undermine your Christian principles and character to leave you limp and helpless, but hold steadfast to your God- given dreams.

Remember God does not make any mistake, He knows where He is taking you. Do not abort your dream, God wants to show you off and show you up. His plan is perfect, 'go for it', do not compromise for compromising is counterfeit. In Genesis 41: 43-46 tells us that Pharaoh also gave Joseph the chariot of his second-in-command, and wherever he went the shout arose, "Kneel down!" And Pharaoh declared to Joseph, "I, the king of Egypt, swear that you shall have complete charge over all the land of Egypt." Pharaoh gave him the name Zaphnathpaaneah meaning "He has the god-like power of life and death!"...He was thirty years old when he entered the service of the king. Joseph went out from the presence of Pharaoh, and began traveling all across the land.

The Psalmist wrote that the Lord God: '… called for a famine on the land of Canaan, cutting off its food supply. Then He sent Joseph as a slave to Egypt to save His people from starvation. There in prison they hurt his feet with fetters, and placed his neck in an iron collar, until God's time finally came – how God tested his patience! Then the king sent for him and set him free. He was put in charge of the king's possessions. At his pleasure he could imprison the king's aides and teach the king's advisors' (Psalm 105: 16-22).

God is checking out your character and your personality, so keep it at a high standard. There was no evidence of guilt that could have stood in Joseph's way for the fulfillment of his dreams; he only knew that one day God would come through for him. This may be so in your case. There are no signs or tags bearing any marks of progress or greatness on you. Your friends, relative, boss or supervisor think they can walk all over you, ignore or disregard you, detest or can't stand you, or even hate you the way Haman hated Mordecai because he did not bow down to him. One day they will respect you when God has repositioned you because of your integrity and faithfulness so hold on to your God given dreams.

Chapter 6

Wait But Don't Procrastinate

During the early stages of a pregnancy, it is easy for a mother to have a miscarriage. The same principle can be applied to your God-given vision; so you need to protect it, nurture it, see that it grows and develops. The enemy would use every demonic power to see that your dreams are destroyed. Even when your vision is of God you will experience disappointment, discouragement and delays.

The truth is, the greater your vision, the greater will be the attack the enemy would advance against you. When you know for certain, deep down in your being that your vision is of God, you will be preserved through hard times as long as you allow the hand of God on your life. You will have the assurance of the Psalmist that: ***'The Lord will work out the plans for my life'*** (Psm.138:8 NLT).

Habakkuk had some complaints in his day (Habakkuk 1&2 TLB). He said, "Wherever I look there is oppression and bribery and men who love to argue and fight. The law is not enforced, no justice is given in the courts, for the wicked far out-number the righteous, and bribes and trickery prevail."

The Lord replied: ***"…look and be amazed! You will be astounded at what I am about to do! I am going to do something in your own lifetime that you will have to see to believe. I am raising a new force on the world scene, the Chaldeans, a cruel and violent nation who will march across the world and conquer it."***

Habakkuk replied, "We are wicked, but they far more (wicked)! You cannot allow sin in any form. Will you stand idly by while they swallow us up? Should you be silent while the wicked destroy those who are better than they? …Will you let them get away with this forever? Will they succeed forever in their heartless wars?" Habakkuk thought he had a legitimate case with God and he was right but God's ways are not our ways, His ways are past finding out.

The Lord said to Habakkuk, ***"Write my answer on a bill board, large and clear, so that anyone can read it at a glance and rush to tell the others. But these things I plan won't happen right away. Slowly, steadily, surely, the time approaches when the vision will be fulfilled. If it seems slow, do not despair, for these things will surely come to pass. Just be patient! They will not be overdue by a single day!"*** That is the way in which God operates, He is God all by Himself, and He does not need our advice on how to act or when He should end our trial.

God is not constricted or restricted to our time in fulfilling the plan for our lives. Many people wear themselves out trying to fulfill a vision God did not give them. It might have been the vision of a grand-mother or a grand-father, parents, one who is their role model or just a person who had some significance in their life at some point in time. It may be their own dream to prove a point, to resolve an issue, to attract attention, to break a record; or it may be just to win a parent's or someone else's love. A word of caution to parents, do not compare your children with any one else, everyone was born with their own individual identity. God will not give them the dream he has for someone else; each person is unique and special, having their own gifting. Also don't expect your children to fulfill your unfulfilled dreams or the dreams you have for them.

The frustration of measuring up with the Jones' or using the yard stick that belongs to someone else will wear you out, so avoid it. Also don't waste your time going out of alignment by doing something which God did not ordain for you less you end up making drastic mistakes and failures and spend so much time and money trying to get back on track. Find out what is God's plan for your life. ***'We are His workmanship created by Christ Jesus unto good works, which God has before ordained that we should walk in them.'*** (Ephesians 2:10 KJV), so you are under construction. Ask the Master Builder, He has the Blue Print for your life and if you think you are not clear and He has not answered as yet, wait. Habakkuk saw some things going on and he asked God and God replied but he had to wait for the answer.

To those who are growing weary and fainting Isaiah 40: 27-31 (TLB) says, ***'O Jacob, O Israel, how can you say that the Lord doesn't see your troubles and isn't being fair? Don't you yet understand? Don't you know by now that the everlasting God, the creator of the farthest parts of the earth, never grows faint or weary? No one can fathom the depths of his understanding. He gives power to the tired and worn out, and strength to the weak. Even the youths shall be exhausted, and the young men will give up. But they that wait on the Lord shall renew their strength. They shall mount up with wings like eagles; they shall run and not be weary; they shall walk and not faint.'*** God has demonstrated a classic example in the life of Abraham that we can learn so much from, here it is:

As recorded in Genesis 15-18 (TLB), God appeared to Abram in a vision and promised him that He will defend him and that He will give him great blessings. Abraham said to God, what are all these blessings to me, if I do not have a son to inherit my wealth or then another member of my household will inherit what I own. God then brought him outside under the night sky and said to him:

"Look up into the heavens and count the stars if you can. Your descendants will be like that, too many to count!" Abram believed God, then God considered him righteous on account of his faith. And He told him, "I am Jehovah, who brought you out of the city of Ur of the Chaldeans, to give you this land forever" (Genesis 15:6-7).

Time went on and Abram and Sarai had no children. Sarai thought that time had run out on them. She said to Abram "Since the Lord has given me no children, you may sleep with my servant girl and her children shall be mine. Abram agreed and Hagar ended up giving birth to Ishmael, through the bad advice of Sarai.

When Abram was ninety-nine years old, God appeared to him and told him, "I am the Almighty; obey me and live as you should (as you ought to). I will prepare a contract between us, guaranteeing to make you into a mighty nation. In fact you shall be the father of not only one nation, but a multitude of nations!" Abram fell face downward in the dust as God talked with him. "What's more, I am changing your name. It is no longer 'Abram' (Exalted Father'), but 'Abraham' (Father of Nations') for that is what you will be. I have declared it. I will give you millions of descendants who will form many nations! Kings shall be among your descendants! ...for it shall be between me and your children as well."

Then God added, "Regarding Sarai your wife-her name is no longer 'Sarai' but 'Sarah' ('Princess'). And I will bless her and give you a son from her! Yes I will bless her richly, and make her the mother of nations! Many kings shall be among your posterity."

Then Abraham threw himself down in worship before the Lord, but inside he was laughing in disbelief! "Me be a father?" he said in amusement. "Me, at 100 years old? And Sarah, to have a baby at 90 years?" (Genesis 17:17 TLB).

This was a promise by God for Abraham and Sarah many years before and God never went back on His promise, He just kept updating it. They could not wait on God, they thought they needed to help God with His plan. The Psalmist says 'they shall bring forth fruit in old age' (Psalm92:14 KJV).

And Abraham said to God, "Yes, do bless Ishmael!"

"No, God replied, "That isn't what I said. Sarah shall bear you a son; and you are to name him Isaac ('Laughter'), and I will sign my covenant with him forever, and with his descendants. As for Ishmael, all right I will bless him also, just as you have asked me to… But my contract is with Isaac, who will be born to you and Sarah next year at about this time."

The Lord does not sanction our acts of deliberate disobedience because they are not lined up with His will. He has made us free moral agents and would not impose His will upon us, but if we ask for His blessing He will give it, in that He will permit and bless it upon your request, but remember there will be consequences that we would encounter soon or later.

The Lord appeared again to Abraham while he was living in the oak grove at Mamre. One hot summer afternoon as he was sitting in the opening of his tent, he suddenly noticed three men coming toward him. He sprang up to meet them and welcomed them and hastily set a meal before them.

"Where is Sarah your wife?" they asked him.

"In the tent" Abraham replied.

Then the Lord said, "Next year I will give you and Sarah a son!" (Sarah was listening from the tent door behind him). Now Abraham and Sarah were both very old, and Sarah was long since past the time when she could have a baby.

So Sarah laughed silently. "A woman my age has a baby?" she scoffed to herself. "And with a husband as old as mine?"

Then God said to Abraham "Why did Sarah laugh? Why did she say 'Can an old woman like me have a baby?' **Is anything too hard for God?** Next year, just as I told you, I will certainly see to it that Sarah has a son."

But Sarah denied it. "I didn't laugh," she lied, for she was afraid.

When you were young, did you ever hear your mother pray or speak to herself and then laugh? You thought she was crazy or she was 'nuts'. No, she was not. She was dreaming of things that were to come forth in the future. It made her happy so she laughed. You asked her about it and she denied that she laughed. That's not all to it. Now that you are grown you find yourself doing the same thing, dreaming about your future and laughing to yourself. You dream of a career, a fine husband or a beautiful wife and nice kids, a well designed house and nice car. Just keep dreaming, take your time and wait on God and your dream would become a reality.

Or are you thinking that your life is finished and done away with? You are saying too many things have gone wrong for me, there will never be any recourse; it is too late, too much water has gone under the bridge of life, you cannot retrace your steps. You are right, what's done cannot be undone. If you are serving the God of the impossible, Jehovah Jireh, your Provider, has a plan for you and you must put your trust and confidence in The

All Wise God and serve Him, He can turn things around for you. He will stem the tide, calm the raging sea, speak to every contrary wind, and to everything that is dormant and dead in your life He can resurrect it, if you ask Him to, so that His plan could be established. Don't forget God asked, "Is anything too hard for God?"

Genesis 21:1-5 says: 'Then God did as He had promised and Sarah became pregnant and give Abraham a baby son in his old age, at the time God had said; and Abraham named him Isaac. You see the Lord is not restricted to human weaknesses and limitations; man's limitations become an opportunity for God to operate.

That's the God we serve. In some people's eyes we are so late to get pregnant with the plan of God, but ***'If God said it He will perform it and if He spoke it he will bring it to pass. He is not a man that He will lie neither is He a man that He will repent'*** (Numbers 23:19). Believe God, He is a covenant-keeping God. He is faithful to His word, just keep on finding out what His plan for your life is, but the timing is in His hand, it is not yours to decide.

Lamentations 3:25 (AMP) says, ***'The Lord is good to those who wait…expectantly for Him'*** When you pray in expectancy it demonstrates your confidence in God regardless to the outcome. It means that you will not fret and take things in your hands; God will honour your faith. Whatever your needs are, pray. Jesus said, ***"It gives your Father great happiness to give you the benefits of his kingdom"*** (Luke 12:32 NLT). God wants to be good to you, so tell him the 'desires of your heart' (Psalm 37:4 NKJV). Thank Him, knowing that the answer will come in His time, not yours.

God could have given Abraham and Sarah their son at an earlier stage of their life but He wanted to exhibit Himself as the powerful God for who He is. Imagine Sarah's hormones becoming active again, her eggs are once again being fertile; her womb which was dormant is again opening up and alive. Her husband Abraham is producing sperms and is also sexually active because they are about to fulfill the prophetic Word of God that has been promised to them for twenty years; that's a long time to wait. No wonder they keep laughing each time they got the Word, the thought of that impossibility made them happy. It is great to be chosen by God to fulfill His calling. Their faith was connected to a hope in God's Word.

'Then God did as He had promised, and Sarah became pregnant and gave Abraham a baby son in his old age, at the time God had said…And Sarah declared, "God has brought me laughter! All who hear about this shall rejoice with me. For who would have dreamed that I would ever have a baby? Yet I have given Abraham a child in his old age!"' The prophetic utterances and signs of our lives must be manifested because God is an unswerving God who fulfills His promises to His people under any circumstances, conditions and the confines of His will.

Who would have thought that Abraham and Sarah would still be able to have a child after so much time had passed but they experienced the fulfillment of God's promise and He kept His Word and did not relinquish His plan for their lives. So if you think that your dream or your prophetic word is taking a long time to be manifested, don't give up, time does not belong to you but it belongs to God, stay focused, revive your trust and faith in an omnipotent, omniscient and an ever-present God.

Romans 4:16-25 (TLB) says:

So God's blessings are given to us by faith, as a free gift; …for Abraham is the father of us all when it comes to these matters of faith. …God made Abraham the father of many nations. God will accept all people in every nation who trust God as Abraham did. And this promise is from God himself, who

makes the dead alive again and speaks of future events with as much certainty as though they were already past.

Abraham believed God even though such a promise just couldn't come to pass! And because his faith was strong, he didn't worry about the fact that he was too old to be a father … and that Sarah was too old to have a baby. Abraham never doubted. He believed God, for his faith and trust grew ever stronger, and he praised God for this blessing even before it happened. And because of Abraham's faith God forgave his sins and declared him 'not guilty.'

Now this wonderful statement – that he was accepted and approved through his faith – wasn't just for Abraham's benefit. It was for us, too, assuring us that God will accept us in the same way he accepted Abraham – when we believe the promises of God who brought back Jesus our Lord from the dead. He died for our sins and rose again to make us right with God, filling us with God's goodness.

So strengthen your faith through the Scriptures. Keep giving God the glory and praise for what He has promised you, knowing that such faith like Abraham's, honours God and God honours such faith. You can begin with the mustard seed faith.

Don't Procrastinate!

If you are thinking that your warranty has expired on God's promise to you, just think again. You maybe find yourself in a state of despondency, wishing your life was different, wishing things had gone the other way. Each day you wallow in self pity, having this pity party all by yourself, shifting blame here and there and not taking any responsibility, it has been like this for a long time now and there seems to be no end to it. How long will you stay in this state of mind? Why are you putting off and canceling your movement in the right direction?

Once Jesus meant everything to you, now it is so different. If Jesus started a good work He can finish it. He that has begun a good work in you is able to complete it unto the day of perfection. No matter how awful things are looking, Jesus can fix it. You have developed some habits which you will like to break because they are not wholesome and you know they are breaking the Father and His son's heart. You are even breaking your loved ones heart; please come back to the Father, His son will lead the way. Don't wait any longer or put it off for another day; in other words, don't procrastinate.

The story is told in Luke 15: 11-32 (TLB) of a man who had two sons and the younger told his father that he wanted his share of the estate instead of waiting until his father was dead. His father agreed and divided his wealth between his two sons. A few days later the younger son packed his belongings and went into a far country and there wasted all his money on parties and riotous living. When all his money was finished and there was a famine in the land, his friends left him, and he was starving. He had to look for a job and the only job he could find was one to feed pigs. He also had to eat the pigs' food as no one gave to him.

He finally came to himself as he realized that his father had many hired servants with bread and enough to spare and he was dying with hunger. He said "I will go home to my father and say 'Father I have sinned against both heaven and you and I am no longer worthy of being called your son. Please take me on as a hired man'."

So he returned home to his father. While he was a long way off his father saw him coming and was filled with loving pity and ran and embraced him and kissed him. He told his father that he was not worthy to be his son, but the father said, "Quick! Bring the finest robe in the house and put the ring on his finger and shoes on his feet, and kill the calf in the fattening pen. We must celebrate with a feast, for this son of mine was dead and has returned to life. He was lost and is found. So the party began.

The prodigal son realized he had made a mistake and he now had to make a conscious decision that he was not going to remain in his state, he was going to act with courage. Nothing happens while you are holding back, get up and give it a try, the Father is waiting to welcome you home. There are times you have to wait for God's direction before you move but when the green light is turned on don't wait or procrastinate. Your situation may never be perfect but step on it. Don't wait for your fears to disappear, they may never go, take the initiative and be brave.

Remember, 'quitters don't win and winners don't quit'. Overcomers know that they have to seize the moment and every opportunity thrown at them. As soon as you start moving forward, some things will become easy and clear. No one can move to a new place unless they leave the old, so don't let your past hold your future in captivity. When you move, God will allow you to gravitate to His will and as time goes on your love and passion for what you are doing will get stronger and many of the problems will take care of themselves.

You must be willing to persevere even though things get rough at times; it would not be smooth sailing all the time. There are times when you will experience sudden storms, gusts of wind or even turbulent seas but that's all right, Jesus Christ is in the ship with you and He is right there at the helm. Keep on asking God to take you through the rough waters, so that you would be always mindful of a powerful God, that when He speaks peace to your wind you will know that it was Him and not you who did it. You must give Him the glory for it and don't take the credit for yourself.

You will always have a testimony of how Jesus brought you through. ***'They overcame by the blood of the lamb and the word of their testimony'*** (Revelation12:11). You will be able to encourage someone else who is behind you, coming through. You also need the experience to help you to learn and grow. There are lessons that are being taught not only in school but on life's journey, on the battlefield and on the race track of life. The race is not for the swift but for those who endure to the end.

There may be some adjustments that may be required, so God has to show you by His divine knowledge and revelation that a shift or relocation or diversion is necessary. He is looking at the bigger picture. We can be hard on the prodigal son but he went out and learnt a valuable lesson. He probably was taking some things for granted but the experience would benefit him for the future. He said, "I will go home to my father." He was willing to admit he made a mistake and to admit his fault to his father.

His action in the pig pen was a good one, any action is better than none at all. Sometimes we can wait too late to make a move. The only way to get rid of a difficult task is to do it. Sometimes we may perceive a task is difficult and when we get into it only to realize that it was easy. Taking action opens the door to opportunities, which can lead to success or failure but if you do nothing, you have failed already. So go ahead, find out from God what sort of decision you should be making. There should be a goal you should be setting or striving to achieve, seize your moment. Solomon writes ***'If you wait for perfect conditions, you will never get anything done'*** (Ecclesiastes 11:4 TLB). It is better to be 80% sure than wait for 100% certain, because by then the opportunity will pass you by.

If you want to obey God's will He gives the commission and the mission, He sets the time of your calling. He dictates the place where you should be at each stage of your life and it is not an accident or coincident, only if you are bent on doing your own thing. Have you received your calling as yet? What is it? If you don't know it or you are not certain, ask God and when He gives you, act on it. It may involve your calling by winning others to

Jesus Christ, which is your task as a parent, winning your friends at school or the workplace, the children in your neighbourhood, being a volunteer at your church. The Psalmist said, ***'My times are in thy hand'*** (Psalm31:15).

In difficult circumstances in life and in times of waiting, we are often refined and mellowed. The things that a young person wants to do or the places they want to go are much different from that of an older person. A young person is more adventurous and pliable and free to make mistakes, an older person cannot afford to be making silly mistakes, they do not have that length of time and energy on their hand to play with, for them time is precious. Whether old or young, manage your time wisely and take advantage of the experiences and lessons along the way, they add value to your life. God's blessing might not be immediate but they will come if we are faithful.

If your life is not going the way you want it to, you are responsible for changing it. God will help you if you turn to Him. But you must want to change, decide to change and work each day towards that change. Do you want to be successful? Then you have to stop putting things off because if you take too long to make up your mind, you might miss an important opportunity, learn to seize every defining moment.

Let a verse of this song from Alvin Slaughter challenge you:

It's time to wake up and make our dreams come true
Time is always moving and it will not wait for you
The fear inside your mind can quench the fire in your heart
Sometimes where you aint is where God wants you to start
It's never easy when you're walking out by faith
Everything looks so different and new
But if we only learn to see with eyes of faith
We would see life in a different view.

Launch out into the deep; let your faith take you somewhere

That you've never been before, launch out into the deep
Let your faith make you fly, let your faith make you soar
Launch out, launch out.

So much for you are waiting, so stop procrastinating
Close your eyes, just take a gleam…

After Jesus had finished preaching to the crowds of people from Simon's boat, He said to Simon "Launch out into the deep and let down your nets for a draught."

Simon said to him "Master, we have toiled all the night, and have taken nothing: nevertheless at thy word I will let down the net." When they did, they enclosed a great multitude of fishes: and their net was breaking (Luke 5: 4-6 KJV).

You might be doing something for months and years but it has not been producing the correct results or no result at all, but one Word from God can change your circumstances and your situation. You have to be in obedience to that Word, because there is life and power in that Word. So launch out by faith and experience a big draught that can change your position. You will be amazed at the life changing impact that Word from God can have on your life, so act on it now.

Chapter 7

Travailing Men And Women Of Zion

There are some situations that are prominent in our societies today. They are a matter of concern and have affected the young people in our nations, especially our young men. It is the cries, groans, moans and travailing of men and women in our villages, towns, cities, societies, and communities that will bring the hearts of the nation's young people back to the Father's love. When are we going to be our brothers' and our sisters' keepers, and fulfill the will of Christ by taking on the burden of caring for them and sharing the love of God to those who are hurting? So often we turn a blind eye and a deaf ear and since it has nothing to do with us, our family or friends it is no concern to us.

These are the days when God is propelling men and women to travail and wail to bring forth hurting men and women. We need to feel the pangs and pain of labour giving birth to organizations, ministries and fulfill the commission and the mission of Jesus

Christ to ***'Go into all the world and preach the Good News to everyone, everywhere'*** (Mark16:15). The good news begins with us, let us win them before the enemy gets them, and let us start with the children. God is depending on you to reap the end-time harvest; we cannot allow Satan to win the battle. Ephesians 6:12 (TLB) says: ***'For we are not fighting against people made of flesh and blood, but against persons without bodies- the evil rulers of the unseen world, those mighty satanic beings and great evil princes of darkness who rule this world and against huge numbers of wicked spirits in the spirit world'.***

Come forth Travailing Men

We have known of situations where a young man would start with one joint of marijuana, offered by his friend. To him it feels good for the first time, because he feels a sense of euphoria and ecstasy. He has never felt better, it gave him a false sense of hope. Before long he is hooked. Later on in life he is not satisfied with a joint of marijuana and needs something stronger and he graduates to maybe coke, crack or crystal-meth. This habit turns out to be very costly but very compelling and so other habits are developed, like stealing and committing other crimes, then he looses his self-esteem and self-worth.

The family he once treasured is neglected, he no longer visits home, only when he needs to harass them for money. His children no longer see him as a dad because he has neglected his responsibility. As a matter of fact, he has been graduated as a gang member and has to live by the rule of the gang. Sometimes he has been beaten mercilessly, especially when he has been sent to sell drugs and did not return with the money. His face has become disfigured with the marks of sin; his life has been threatened at times. He has now become an established perpetrator of the law and before long would be caught. He was often seen on the street like a 'bum' taking rescue and shelter on the sidewalks at nights.

It happened one night as he tried to break into a jewel store with some other gang members, they did not see the police men who were lurking around, and he was shot twice but luckily was not killed. He is now in prison serving a sentence of six years. He has a lot of time now on his hand to regret and to think of where he went wrong. As he looked back on his life fifteen years ago, he had such a promising future ahead of him, every thing looked so good, a career, a nice family, pleasant friends, a good paying job, just started paying for his home.

Now that he is being rehabilitated and all the drugs have worn off, his life of the past flashed before him. 'It is a hell of a nightmare,' he thought. 'This have to be a crude joke, this could not be real, and it is not funny either, this is a dream from which I would soon wake up and find myself back at home with my family'. He shakes himself and has to admit he has made some serious errors and blunders and there is no way in which he could retrace his steps, it is much too late now.

Young man, you may have been incarcerated, friends have forsaken you, parents and relatives have abandoned you. You have tried drugs and alcohol, society cast you off. Your spouse has rejected you, your children do not know you any more. You feel like you are at the end of your rope and you cannot make it any more in life and you are thinking of jumping off somewhere and committing suicide. Listen now, don't, that's what the devil wants. There is still hope for you. Jesus shed His blood and bore your anguish and frustrations so that you can go free. That emptiness or void can be filled by giving Jesus a chance in your life, He can heal your broken heart and set you free from sin and give you a band new life, just commit your life to Jesus now, and He will turn your life around.

We need travailing men to go after these young men to unite them back to the Heavenly Father because they have fallen out of grace and left their first love. Where are these travailing men today? There is so much fear existing in the heart of man today; fear of the economy, of family separation, the lack of finance, not knowing who to trust, not knowing what the future holds, and how long will one live, fear of sickness, would one face an untimely death? Men, you need to groan and mourn when our youths are gunned down and stabbed for drugs, when there is tribal and gang rivalry and disputes, travail to save the nation's children and young people before the devil snatches them away to a Christ-less eternity. The pain is not just for the women but for the men also. Hear what Jeremiah 30:5-9 TLB had to say:

"Where shall we find peace?" they cry. "There is only fear and trembling. Do men give birth? Then why do they stand there, ashen-faced, hands pressed against their sides like women in labour?" Alas, in all history when has there ever been a time of terror such as in that coming day? It is a time of trouble for my people – for Jacob – such as they have never known before. Yet God will rescue them! For on that day, says the Lord of Hosts, I will break the yoke from their necks and snap their chains …For they shall serve the Lord their God …

We are living in a time when the fathers who should take their rightful place as priest in the homes are not there. They are having other relationships, snared in holes, in prison houses, turned to drugs, homosexuality, alcohol and other evils of this life. We need men with vision to start dreaming for these men to bring them back to their original and rightful place in the homes and in the society. Start feeling the pains like women in labour and pray and travail and bring these men through, God is counting on you men to cry out for these lost men.

There are more single parents, where mothers alone are raising their children because fathers have not assumed their role and set godly examples. Fathers, get back to your role and rightful place; you have been weighed in the balance (scale) and found wanting. In other words you have not measured up; you need to take on some more responsibility. God promised that He will break the chains and the bondages and they will return to their Lord. Travailing men, you only need to cry out and travail for God to set them free.

Travailing men, pray and speak positive things back into their lives, see them going back to school, taking up positions in the job markets, rebuilding their lives and their homes, taking their family back to church, going on holidays with their family and going on to giving their testimonies of where God took them from to where they are now. It can happen, so infuse life back into them with your prayer, the Word and your encouragement.

Eli fails to travail

Here is a vivid example, of Eli and his sons, who were weighed in the balances and found wanting (recorded in 1Samuel 2-4). Eli was the priest at the Tabernacle at Shiloh. His sons Hophni and Phinehas didn't love the Lord. It was their regular practice to send out a servant whenever anyone was offering a sacrifice, and while the flesh of the sacrificed animal was boiling, the servant would put a three-pronged flesh hook into the pot and demand that whatever it brought up be given to Eli's sons. They treated all of the Israelites in this manner when they came to worship.

Sometimes the servant will come even before the rite of the burning of the fat on the altar had been performed, and he would demand raw meat before it was boiled, so that it could be used for roasting. The person offering the sacrifice might suggest to the servant to take as much meat as he wanted, except for the fat must be burned (what the law required), but the servant would say, "No, give it to me now or I'll take it by force." So the sin of these young men was very great in the eyes of the Lord; for they treated the people's offering to the Lord with contempt.

Eli was now very old, but he was aware of what was going on around him. He knew for instance, that his sons were seducing the young women who assisted at the entrance of the Tabernacle. Eli told his sons "I have been hearing terrible reports from the Lord's people about what you are doing. It is an awful thing to make the Lord's people sin. Ordinary sin receives heavy punishment, but how much more is this sin of yours which has been committed against the Lord?" But they would not listen to their father, for the Lord was already planning to kill them.

One day a prophet came to Eli and gave him a message from the Lord: "Why have you honoured your sons more than me – for you and they have become fat from the best of the offerings of my people! I will put an end to your family, so that your family will no longer serve as priests. Every member will in future, die before his time. None shall live to be old. You will envy the prosperity I will give my people, but you and your family will be in distress and need.

Those who are yet alive will live in sadness and grief and their children shall die by the sword. And to prove what I have said will come true, I will cause your two sons Hophni and Phinehas, to die on the same day! Then I will raise up a faithful priest who will serve me and do whatever I tell him to do. I will bless his descendants, and his family shall be priests to my kings forever." Meanwhile little Samuel was helping the Lord by assisting Eli in the temple.

Could you imagine, Eli did not rebuke his sons, he stood by as his sons disrespected the house of God. Let us pray for our children and rebuke them when they are wrong or God would hold us responsible. God also spoke to young Samuel concerning Eli's sons saying they were blaspheming Him and Eli did not stop them. The Lord kept His word because later when Israel was at war with the Philistines, they defeated Israel, so they came up with the idea that they would get the Ark of the Lord out of Shiloh and Hophni and Phinehas accompanied it into the battle.

The Philistines panicked at first, but then they fought desperately hard and as a result thirty thousand men of Israel died that day and the remainder fled to their tents. The ark of God was captured and Eli's sons were killed also. A man from the tribe of Benjamin ran from the battle and arrived at the temple of Shiloh the same day with his clothes torn and dirt on his head. Eli was waiting beside the road to hear the news of the battle, for his heart trembled for the safety of the Ark of God.

As the messenger from the battlefront arrived, there was a great cry out of the city. "What is all this noise about?" Eli asked. The messenger told all that had happened (Eli was ninety-eight years old and was blind), Eli fell backward from his seat beside the gate and his neck was broken by the fall and he died (for he was old and fat). He had judged Israel for forty years. Samuel, Hannah's son, took his place. Hannah, who had prayed and fasted and travailed for a son and God answered her prayer. Samuel became one of Israel's greatest prophets. He was a man of prayer who finished the work of the judges, began the school of the prophets and anointed Israel's first King and he grew in wisdom.

God will hold leaders responsible, in the house of God or in the homes, when they do not take on their responsibility and their roles of authority. Eli knew his sons were evil but he did little to correct them, even when the integrity of God's sanctuary was threatened. If Eli had spent more time praying he would have been able to discern what was going on in the Tabernacle. He was not even hearing from God any more. There are times when serious problems must be confronted, even if the consequences might be painful.

If you are in a position of authority, don't rationalize and compromise God's standards for the wrong reasons. God expects leaders to lead fairly and to eliminate evil practices. He will not overlook those who justify their own sins. God wants us to be faithful in our service to Him. When He gives us a job to do, whether in our family, church, community or career; let us do it faithfully or God may find someone else to do it. So, travail men of God and bring forth other children, young men and older men for the kingdom of God. He is depending on you.

Can you feel the pains that Satan caused these men to go through because of pride, greed, wrong up-bringing, lack of proper parenthood? Do not say I am not responsible; I did not bring these people into the world or cause their pain. We know that but God is depending on you, like Mordecai, who saved the king's life when he discovered the threat and intervened. You can do it: labour and travail to bring them to a saving knowledge of Jesus Christ, if they are backslidden, pray them back into the kingdom of God, that Satan would lose the battle on their lives.

Esther travails for the life of her people

Esther became the wife of the Persian king Ahasuerus, after his previous wife, queen Vashti bluntly refused his request during a party held at the palace by king Ahasuerus for his servants and officials. On the final day when the king was half drunk from wine, he told his personal aides to bring queen Vashti to him with the royal crown upon her head so that he can gaze upon her beauty; for she was a beautiful woman, but she refused to go. The king was furious and consulted his lawyers who told him to get rid of queen Vashti, because women everywhere would begin to disobey their husbands. Vashti was then banished from the palace and another queen had to be chosen, one more worthy than Vashti.

Mordecai, a Jew, had been captured when Jerusalem was destroyed by king Nebuchadnezzar and had been exiled to Babylon. He had a beautiful young cousin Hadassah (also called Esther), whose father and mother were dead, and whom he had adopted into his family and raised as his own daughter. Now because of the king's decree Esther was brought to the King's harem at Shushan palace, along with many other girls.

Hegai, who was responsible for the harem, was very much impressed with Esther and did his best to make her happy. He ordered special menus for her, favoured her for the beauty treatments, gave her seven girls from the palace for her maids, and also the most luxurious apartment in the harem. When favour is on your life there is no telling how far God can take you. Sometimes it seems as though it is not fair but God bestows it according to His will, His design and plan.

Esther hadn't told anyone that she was a Jew for Mordecai had said she must not. He came daily to the court to find out what was happening to her. Each girl was given six months beauty treatment and would spend one night with the king. Esther was to be given her choice of clothing or jewelry that she wished to enhance her beauty with. Next morning she would return to the second harem where the king's wives lived.

When it was Esther's turn to go to the king, she accepted the advice of Hegai, dressing according to his instructions. All the other girls exclaimed with delight when they saw her. So Esther was taken to the king's palace. The king loved Esther more than any of the other girls. He was so delighted with her that he set the royal crown on her head and declared her queen instead of Vashti.

Soon afterwards king Ahasuerus appointed Haman as Prime Minister. He was the most powerful official in the empire next to the king himself. All the king's officials bowed before him, except Mordecai, being a Jew. The others spoke to Haman about it and he was furious. He decided he would deal with it by asking the king to issue a decree because this certain race of people ought to be destroyed because they did not obey the king's laws. He would put $20,000 into the treasury for this purpose.

The king agreed, giving him his ring as confirmation, telling him, "Go ahead and do as you like with these people." So letters were sent out in this regard. When Mordecai learned what had been done, he tore his clothes and put on sack cloth and ashes and went out into the city, crying with a loud and bitter wail. Great mourning went out among the Jews, fasting and weeping. Esther heard of it and sent clothes for Mordecai. He sent a copy of the king's decree for Esther and requested that she should go to the king to plead for her people. Her reply was that she could not enter the king's court without his permission and if he didn't hold up his golden scepter, for her, she would die.

Mordecai's reply to Esther was, "Do you think you will escape there in the palace, when all other Jews are killed? If you keep quiet at a time like this God will deliver the Jews from some other source, but you and your relatives will die. What's more, who can say, but that God has brought you into the palace for such a time as this?"

Esther sent a message back to Mordecai saying, "Go and gather all the Jews of Shushan and fast for me; do not eat or drink for three days, night or day and I and my maids will do the same. I will go in to see the king and if I perish, I perish." So Mordecai did as Esther told him. We know from the rest of the account that God orchestrated the incidents that followed, which saved the lives of the Jewish people.

As Mordecai correctly stated, we are in God's kingdom so that we can effectively make some changes. When things go wrong all around us do we turn a blind eye; or do we say whatever is to happen will happen? Or do we try to effect changes? When we think that we do not have solutions to the problems we fast and pray and God would intervene and bring victory.

Vashti failed so that a vacancy was created for Esther, who was divinely appointed by God; for He knew that somewhere down the road it was going to take a person of prominence to save the lives of the Jews. It was also appropriate that Mordecai raised Esther the correct way in the fear of the Lord, that when disaster or crisis struck she knew that prayer and fasting moves the hand of God. When he asked her to go to the king, she did not understand her calling, so Mordecai had to explain it to her. In other words, 'This is why God placed you there to make a difference, to change things or to cause things to happen, to save lives.' She met the criteria of the worthy position of queen and with it came the influence, in that she was able to convince her maidens and the king.

Mordecai travailed too, he first started the wail. Being in the palace as an official, he was aware of the plans and laws. God sets us up in strategic positions and places for his purposes not just to fatten ourselves like Eli and his sons but to look out for our brothers and sisters. We need not shirk our responsibility but to fulfill our role according to God's purpose and destiny.

Come forth travailing men and women of Zion

When men and women of Zion travail, sons and daughters will come forth, Satan is defeated and the kingdom of God is elevated. The labour pains and the intensity of the heat of passionate plight send us straight into labour and push us into our destiny. When the people come together in prayer the manifestation of the power of God must take place. Micah 4: 9 (NIV) states '***Why do you cry aloud and have you no king in you? Has your counselor perished, that pain seizes you like that of a woman in labour? Writhe in agony, O daughter of Zion, like a woman in labour … Arise and thresh, O daughter***

of Zion, for I will give you horns of iron; I will give you hoofs of bronze and you will break to pieces many nations."

First of all, the prophet Micah is asking some important questions that we are not to make light of. Why are you screaming? Do you have a king resonating in you? In other words, where is your God? Where is the One who should be giving you counsel, advice and guidance? Then why are you in pain like a woman in labour? You twist and squirm as though you are in agony because of what is going on inside of you... Then arise: speak out, pray against, wage spiritual war, destroy, plunder, attack, and break down the forces of hell. 'I will give you instruments to compel the powers of darkness to disappear and to pull down Satan's kingdom, not only in your nation but in many nations'.

God will give us a tenacity and a boldness to fight for our children, other people's children, our friends and extended family, the people in different institutions, and the Governments in our nations, so that the devil's plans and strategies would be defeated and come to nothing. Travailing men and women will birth prophetic movements of God that will save communities and nations, set the people free from the tyranny and bondages of generational curses. If we do not pray and travail then God cannot move on our behalf, when we pray we move the hand of God.

Men can come forth from the place of degradation and demoralization, out of the mire of sin to a place of restoration with the King. You can be delivered from your past life to one of son-ship with Jesus Christ. He can turn your life around, just acknowledge where you went wrong and repent, He can lift your standard once again and break the shackles and bondages off your life, clean you up and give you a new life, with different goals, purpose and values with high expectations and ideals. He can do it, just give Him the chance. God will restore your health, happiness, finance, family, stability and stamina.

Daughter of Zion, as you travail for the right cause, God will reward you in due season. You are standing up for a just cause; you are believing God for a turnaround of lives, even if you have to stand alone. You were not like this all the time, but you have experienced some challenging times that have changed your life and opened your eyes and now you have joined the fight. You do not have much support and backing but you are doing it because you know where God has brought you from. You don't feel comfortable seeing people going through what you went through. As you walk tall and hold your head up high, they are thinking, 'Who does she think she is, pouncing herself around like that?' They know your past but they do not know your future, they do not know where the King is taking you. That's ok. Let them treat you with scorn and disdain now, the time is coming when you are going to shine, Daughter of Zion.

"I do not have a house now but the King promises me one, a car is coming too, I may have had a husband who was not belonging to me, but the King says I am going to have one of my own. If my friends could only see what I am visioning they would never shun me but I will cope with it because my time is coming some day, I do not know when but time is in the King's hand. He is a Just King; He says that I only have to remain faithful. He says nothing good will He withhold from me when I walk uprightly. So give Him praise and glory, for he is the King of Kings and Lord of Lords".

Chapter 8

WHO'S IN THE HOUSE

We all have equal value in God's eyes, but we don't have equal giftedness. You may be aware of your abilities, and feel good about yourself, having previously achieved success and lots of accomplishments. Please take note that your talent was given by God and it is your duty to develop it, so don't beat your chest as though you did it all on your own. Give some credit and praise to the Great I Am. If you are seeking to be God's ideal, keep looking to Him to enhance the talent or talents he has given to you, and not the one you think you want or you would be wasting your time. For example don't try to be a Lawyer when your calling is to be a Doctor.

If you have fallen short of your life expectations, work on bringing them to a higher level. If your character needs enhancement, try to make some adjustments; you must never stop working on your areas of weakness. In other words, to fulfill your God-given assignment, you must recognize your strength and go for it. ***'Much is required from those to whom much is given, for their responsibility is greater'*** (Luke 12:48 TLB). Great gifting means great responsibility! God distributes His talents, knowledge, wisdom and ability to a man or woman whom He sees fit.

There is no higher calling than to be called by God for a task or an assignment. At the same time, the higher the calling, the more humble you must become. If you believe you are called for a higher calling in Jesus Christ or for a greater work, you just fall on your knees and on your face before God and ask for His guidance. You will need Him on the journey. Those who exalt themselves are humbled by the Lord and those who humble themselves before the Lord are raised by the Lord.

We have seen the hand of God working mightily on the lives of those whom God has chosen from their humble state and raised them up to be great leaders in different fields of the world. You might be feeling discouraged, thinking that God has forgotten you because the enemy has off-loaded some stuff on you and has been doing that for the longest while. As long as you know that God has a plan for you, just be encouraged as He continues to check your life. Keep on walking clean and pure before Him. Don't step out of line because the moment you do, it may be the very moment He is about to move in your life, so stay on guard. Disregard the enemy and bind the forces of hell.

There may be a situation where you know of someone who has been going through a tough time, being maligned all the time. They have been told that they would not amount to anything, they looked so insignificant and has been called all sorts of names; being cursed with spells and aspersions. We need to be careful, for whom God blesses no man curses. Man does not determine whom God must bless; it is His decision to make.

What He speaks over your life, He is committed to stand by it. He is not man that He would lie.

God disposes whenever He wishes and predestines by His foreknowledge, He chooses whom He desires and He is not impartial, but He favours at His will for He is God Almighty and Sovereign Lord. Regardless of how we may judge a person, God has the final say. There comes a time when God will say, "This is the time for you to rise, move up, be promoted and fulfill your purpose for which I have created you." Who are we to say, "Why God?" We never know sometimes 'who is in our house'. Check these worthy gentlemen out:

"Let my people go"

It is recorded in the book of Exodus that there was a time in Egypt when a new Pharaoh came to power and he felt no obligation to Joseph's descendants. He thought that the Israelites were becoming too powerful and dangerous because they were so many. So the Egyptians made them slaves and put brutal taskmasters over them. But the more they mistreated and oppressed them, the more they multiplied. He then instructed the Hebrew midwives to kill all the baby boys and let the girls live. The midwives, having a fear of God refused to do it. He then commanded all of his people to throw the newborn Hebrew boys into the Nile River to be eaten by crocodiles.

This was when a mother saw that she had an unusual baby and decided she could not let her baby die but made a waterproofed basket, put the baby in it and laid it at the river's edge and had his sister guard it. Pharaoh's daughter came to bathe, saw the basket, opened it, and there was the baby crying. This touched her heart; the baby's sister came and asked if she could get a Hebrew woman to nurse the baby for her. The princess agreed and the mother of the baby came and she said, "I will pay you well!" So the mother took him home and nursed him. When the mother brought the baby back to Pharaoh's daughter she called him Moses, meaning 'to draw out' because she had drawn him out of the water.

If God has designed your life for greatness, the devil would be after you to destroy you and he would not give up but God will protect you because there is a purpose why you are alive. He gave Moses' mother the discernment that he was a special child and the wisdom of how to protect him and where to take him. Herod wanted to kill baby Jesus but an angel of the Lord appeared to Joseph telling him to flee to Egypt until the Lord brought him word again.

So Moses grew up in the palace and attended some of the best universities and colleges in Egypt at Pharaoh's expense. All this training was necessary for the assignment that God had for him. It was soon time for him to leave the grandeur of the palace. He was now a man and went out for a visit to his fellow Hebrews and saw an Egyptian knock a fellow Hebrew to the ground. Moses looked this way and that, when he thought that no one was watching, he killed the Egyptian and hid his body in the sand. Pharaoh found out and ordered his arrest but he ran away to Midian through the wilderness.

He was forty years at the time. He thought that he was bringing justice to a people who were treated with injustice, but he went about it the wrong way, so God had to teach him some lessons. He showed Moses that by doing things his own way he couldn't keep a single soldier buried in the sand. By doing things God's way, a whole army could be buried in the depths of the Red Sea. He took him out of his comfort zone to chip away some anger and hurt.

He married a priest of Midian's daughter. He was now a shepherd but under the guidance of Jethro, his father-in-law. What a humbling experience running from Pharaoh for his life, coming through the wilderness to Midian, from a Prince to a shepherd. He is now learning about life in the wilderness, cultures and behaviours of people, how to control his anger and the will of the Spirit through the ministry of his father-in-law Jethro, who was a priest. He needed this training for the journey ahead through the wilderness. God was shaping him to stand before Pharaoh to demand that he let the people go.

Do you feel at times that you are oppressed by your enemy? All you need to do is cry out to Jesus. Do not take things in your own hands, do it God's way. The Lord says, "Justice belongs to me; I will repay them." He also said, "The Lord himself will handle these cases." It is a fearful thing to fall into the hands of the Living God (Hebrews10:30).

The road to fulfilling God's purpose is not an easy one. Sometimes the rug is pulled from under your feet, or you might experience a sudden drop from top to bottom but when God is ready to raise you up, no man can bring you down. He makes you deal with your malice, greed, and other vices. He can equip you with what is necessary for you to make your calling a success. Do not despise the training you receive in the backside of your desert or wilderness, this is preparing you for your entrance before nobles or for greater battles and victories.

Moses' attention was drawn to a burning bush that was not being consumed. He went over to investigate, then God spoke to him out of the burning bush and told him to take his shoes off because he was standing on holy ground. He said:

"I am the God of Abraham, Isaac and Jacob. I have seen the deep sorrows of my people in Egypt and have heard their pleas for freedom from their task masters. I have come to deliver them and to take them out of Egypt into a good land, a large land, a land flowing with milk and honey. Yes, the wail of the people of Israel has risen to me in heaven, and I have seen the heavy tasks the Egyptians have oppressed them with. Now I am

going to send you to Pharaoh, to demand that he let you lead my people out of Egypt."

The first excuse that Moses made was, "I am not the person for the job." God told him, "I will certainly be with you and this is the proof that when you lead the people out of Egypt, you shall worship on this mountain."

The next question he posed to God was, "Which God should I say to the Israelites sent me?" To this God replied, "… say to the children of Israel, 'I AM has sent me to you! Jehovah, the God of your ancestors Abraham, Isaac and Jacob has sent me to you.' The elders of the people of Israel will accept you. They will go with you to the king of Egypt …"

Moses' other excuse was, "They won't believe me! They won't do what I tell them to. They'll say, 'Jehovah never appeared to you!'" God had to show him a sign by the shepherd's rod that he was using, in that when he threw it down the rod became a serpent. This was going to be a symbol, which he was to use on many occasions.

The next excuse was that he was not a good speaker because he had an impediment. To this the Lord became angry and said, "All right, your brother is a good speaker, he is coming here today, I will help both of you to speak." God will call you to do the very thing that you are passionate about. Moses wanted to rescue that Israelite from the Egyptian and that was what God was calling him to do, as a matter of fact God had already placed that passion in him.

Are you making excuses when God has appointed you for an assignment? Does God have to show you signs and wonders before you tell Him that you are compliant and obedient? He has already given you the qualification, experience and the confirmation that He has chosen you, but you still have not made a move. You are waiting and questioning God. The Lord had already chosen Moses as an ambassador to Pharaoh; he was to use the rod in his hand to bring forth signs and wonders in Egypt. What do you have in your hand to bring forth some miraculous accomplishment for God's glory? Like Moses you have what it takes but you are still questioning God. You have in your hand your gifts, money, temperament, experience, relationships, your mind, education; these are strengths not weaknesses, so use them.

Moses was eighty years old and Aaron was eighty-three at the time of their confrontation with Pharaoh. Moses was so discouraged at times but God used him and the rod to demonstrate God's power and to stand before Pharaoh. The rod ate Pharaoh's rod, it brought ten plagues on the Egyptians, it parted the Red Sea, and Moses used it to strike the rock for the Israelites to get water. Moses turned out to be one of the greatest leaders in his time. He led millions of Israelites out of Egypt. A nation was born because he refused to stop the struggle to achieve his divine destiny: to lead his people out of bondage and free them from Pharaoh's oppression.

The report in Hebrews 11: 24-26 (TLB) states, 'It was by faith that Moses, when he grew up, refused to be treated as the grandson of the king, but chose to share ill-treatment with God's people instead of enjoying the fleeting pleasures of sin. He thought that it was better to suffer for the promised Christ than to own all the treasures of Egypt, for he was looking forward to the great reward that God would give him.'

Who would have guessed while Moses was in the palace that he would be the one to deliver the children of Israel? Pharaoh and his household did not know who was in the house. He was God's under-cover leader. He knew who Pharaoh was, he knew of his strategies and knew how wicked he was, that's why he ran from him and was afraid to go back to Egypt. When the training was finished he was ready and filled with confidence, to fill the capacity as leader and to challenge Pharaoh with what God said, "Let my people go."

There are times when we have to let go the ways of the world so that we can answer to the call of God. What is it that you have in terms of an instrument, or an ability that God has given you that He can use? He can only use it when you yield it and your life, so bring it as an offering and appreciation of what His son Jesus Christ did for you. In time you too can say to the devil, that God says, **"Let my people go."**

From a shepherd to a king

As it is recorded in 1Samuel 16-17, God said to Samuel, "You have mourned long enough for Saul, for I have rejected him as king of Israel. Now take a vial of olive oil and go to Bethlehem and find a man named Jesse, for I have selected one of his sons to be the new king."

But Samuel asked, "How can I do that? If Saul hears about it he will kill me."

The Lord replied, "Take a heifer with you and say that you have come to make a sacrifice to the Lord. Then call Jesse to the sacrifice and I will show you which of his sons to anoint."

So Samuel went and performed the purification rite and invited Jesse and his sons. When they arrived, Samuel took one look at Eliab and thought, 'Surely this is the man the Lord has chosen!'

But the Lord said to Samuel "Don't judge by a man's face or height, for this is not the one. I don't make decisions the way you do! Men judge by outward appearance but I look at a man's thoughts and intentions."

Next to pass before Samuel was Abinadab. The Lord said, "No, this is not the one." In the same way all seven sons presented themselves to Samuel and were rejected. The Lord has not chosen any of them," Samuel told Jesse, "Are these all?"

"Well, there is the youngest," Jesse replied, "but he's out in the fields watching the sheep." At this time this son was so insignificant that he was not even numbered among the brothers.

"Send for him at once," Samuel said, "for we will not sit down to eat until he arrives." So Jesse sent for him. He was a fine looking boy, ruddy-faced, and with pleasant eyes. And the Lord said, "This is the one; anoint him."

Don't you like that when we are being overlooked God is looking down on us. He picks us for his special tasks, that is God's favour and it has nothing to do with man's choice. David was just a shepherd boy, not much education is required for that, it is a humble beginning. When Jesus Christ was born, the angels appeared to shepherds to tell them the good news first. They are a people that are generally looked down on but God has them in a special category. No wonder David regards the ***'Lord is a good Shepherd, and I have everything I need, He lets me rests in the meadows green, and leads me besides the quiet stream. He restores my failing health. He helps me do what honours Him the most'*** (Psalm23:1-3 TLB).

David stood there among his brothers. Samuel took the olive oil he had brought and poured it upon David's head; and the spirit of Jehovah came upon him and gave him great power from that day onward. God is ready to pour out His spirit upon you as in the day of Pentecost; you only need to desire the anointing of God. He will anoint you to do the things He has called you to do. It does not matter what the job is, He will give you the grace and the anointing to do it.

David's first assignment was to go to the palace and play his harp for King Saul, to help him calm his evil spirit. When the Lord sent a tormenting spirit upon Saul, one of his aides suggested a harp player. He said he knew a young fellow in Bethlehem, the son of Jesse, who was not only a talented harp player but was handsome, brave and strong and had good solid judgment. ***'A man's gift makes room for him, and brings him before great men'*** (Proverbs 18:16 Amp.). He used to play in the fields as a shepherd. That was a wonderful testimony to start out with.

From the moment Saul saw David he loved him; and David became his bodyguard. Then Saul wrote to Jesse, "Please let David join my staff, for I am very fond of him." Whenever the tormenting spirit from God troubled Saul, David would play the harp and Saul would feel better and the spirit would go away. Saul had no idea that it would be this same person playing for him would replace him on the throne one day. He did not have a clue 'who is in the house'. When his evil spirit would come on him at times and he tried to kill David, the anointing and the calling on David's life blocked or redirected every javelin.

David's next assignment was when he killed Goliath, a Philistine champion from Gath, who came out of the Philistine ranks to face the forces of Israel. He was a giant measuring over nine feet tall. He had the army of Israel paralyzed because none of them dared to face this giant to fight him. David said, "Don't worry about a thing; I'll take care of this Philistine!" Saul gave him his armour but he refused to use it. Even though a king gives you his armour, it does not mean that you have to wear it: what fits others might not fit you. Follow God's directions and leadings.

David took his staff in his hand, picked up five smooth stones from a stream and putting them in his shepherd's bag and with his sling, he went towards Goliath. "Am I a dog," he reared at David, "that you come at me with a stick?" And he cursed David by the names of his gods. "Come over here and I'll give your flesh to the birds and wild animals," Goliath yelled.

David shouted in reply, "You come to me with a sword and a spear, but I come to you in the name of the Lord of the armies of heaven and of Israel; the very God whom you have defied. Today the Lord will conquer you and I will kill you and cut off your head; and then I will give the dead bodies of your men to the birds and wild animals, and the whole world will know that there is a God in Israel! And Israel will learn that the Lord does not depend on weapons to fulfill his plans –He works without regard to human means! He will give you to us!" David knew the power of the God he was serving, what a testimony!

As Goliath approached, David ran out to meet him and reaching into his shepherd's bag, took out a stone, hurled it from his sling and hit the Philistine giant in the forehead. The stone sank in and he fell on his face to the ground. So David conquered the Philistine giant with a sling and a stone. He ran over and pulled Goliath's sword from its sheath and killed him with it, then cut off his head. When the Philistines saw that their champion was dead, they turned and ran. The Israelites gave a great shout of triumph and rushed after the Philistines, chasing them as far as Gath and the gates of Ekron. The bodies of the dead and wounded Philistines were strewn all along the road. Then the Israelite army returned and plundered the deserted Philistine camp.

David knew the God he was serving. He had faith in him and therefore he was able to make a bold announcement and confession. Saul and his army were depending on their weapons but David's trust was in the Living God. ***'The name of the Lord is a strong tower, the righteous run into it and they are saved'*** (Proverbs 18: 10 NKJV). David went with confidence because he knew that he could not have done it in his strength but in the might and strength of the Holy One of Israel. David also had the anointing working on his behalf. The army was seeing demise by their spirit of fear but David was seeing the death of Goliath by faith. The velocity and accuracy of the shot had to be measured by the power of God; He is perfect in all His ways.

How much strength and power do you attribute to God? Is He all powerful to conquer every giant in your life? You may be wrestling with some stuff in your life and you may be trying to conquer them in your strength, therefore it is causing you to fail. Give it up and let God have His way. Whatever you do, do it in the strength of the Lord and like David be an over-comer and a conqueror.

When the Israelites were returning home, the women came out from the entire town along the way to celebrate and cheer King Saul and were singing and dancing for joy with tambourines and cymbals. “Saul has slain his thousands and David his ten thousands!” Saul was angry with jealousy and this was the beginning of a long and arduous journey for David fleeing and hiding in caves from Saul who pursued him and wanted to kill him. Again he could not kill him because of the anointing and divine call on his life.

David was continually hounded down by his enemies, but instead of losing faith in God’s promise, David understood that, ‘The Lord has set apart the godly man for Himself; the Lord hears when I call to Him’ (Psalm 4:3 NAS). He declared, ‘In peace I will…lie down and sleep for thou alone, O Lord, make me to dwell in safety’ (Psalm4:8 NAS). When the Philistines captured him he prayed ‘When I am afraid, I will trust in You’ (Psalm 56:3 NAS). When he ended up in a cave while fleeing from Saul’s jealous rage he said, ‘O God, be gracious to me, for my soul takes refuge in Thee; and in the shadow of thy wings I will take refuge until destruction passes by’ (Psalm 57:1 NAS). He says, ‘Our help is in the name of the Lord, who made heaven and earth’ (Psalm124:8 KJV). Eventually Saul was killed in battle and David succeeded Saul to the throne.

During David's reign, he fought many battles; he built many cities and a palace. He became greater and greater, for the Lord God was with him and blessed his kingdom in a mighty way because he wanted to pour out his kindness on Israel, his chosen people. He always inquired of God what he should do and when he succeeded he gave the credit to God. So David moved from a shepherd to a king. His testing and trials were not easy but he persevered and was victorious.

If you are destined to achieve great accomplishments in life be certain that you will start with small achievements first. In other words, you will have to go through small doors before the big ones are opened for you. Before you become captain of ten thousands, you will have to first learn to lead a few sheep in a wilderness or a meadow some where. It does not matter who doesn't recognize you, once God has His eyes on you, you are a marked man or woman with purpose.

If you are 'in the house' where God has chosen for you, no matter what you are going through right now just: ***'Trust in the Lord with all thy heart and lean not unto your own understanding. In all your ways acknowledge Him and he will direct your path'*** (Proverbs 3: 5&6 KJV). Learn to listen to your heart and hear the voice of the Lord. The still, small voice is talking to you ***'...listen to the Lord's instruction'*** (Isaiah 30:10). God has custom-designed you for what He wants you to do; for your ability would reveal your destiny! ***'...If anyone ministers, let him do it as of the ability which God supplies; that God in all things may be glorified through Jesus Christ, to whom be praise and dominion for ever and ever...'***(1Peter 4: 11 NKJV).

When God gives an assignment, He gives the expertise along with it, whether it is the love for figures, computers, art, designing, interior decorating, the talented voice that you have been gifted with; or the ease at which the music comes, naturally, when others find it difficult; the culinary arts, where you said I was just born for this; the talent of writing or dancing; those things that you have done well consistently or what you just enjoy doing. Don't worry about skills you don't have, don't covet strengths that others have, just maximize the gifts that God has blessed you with.

The legend is told that Saint Peter was escorting another saint of God who had made it to heaven, and Peter was giving him a tour of heaven. He showed him beautiful mansions and all the beauties his eyes could behold. There were different mansions with names on them with different size and other variations. He came upon a particular room and the saint asked "What is this one, can I go in there? Peter said "No, you would not want to go in there because you would not want to see what is in there." But the saint insisted that he wanted to, so reluctantly Peter opened the door and they went inside.

As they got inside, there were all sorts of wrapped packages and boxes of different sizes that were unopened with tags on them. They saint asked, "Why are all these packages and boxes here not opened and were not collected by their owners?" To this Peter replied, "They were delivered to their owners but they were not accepted." The saint further asked "Is there one for me?" Peter replied, "Yes, there are many."

Are you one of those people who were given gifts and you did not accept them so they went back to heaven as unclaimed gifts with your name tag still attached? Accept your gift today and work diligently to achieve your destiny. Paul said to Timothy ***'…I remind you to fan into flame the gift of God, which is in you…'*** (2Timothy1:6 NIV). Start fanning the flames of your designs that God has endowed upon you, now.

Chapter 9

WHEN THE ODDS ARE AGAINST YOU

THE STRUGGLE IS NOT EASY

Let us look at a typical example of a successful life. The journey has been 'smooth sailing', having succeeded in your academics, with passes of distinction, which placed you in the bracket of an exceptional scholar. You therefore have a bright future ahead, because you are deemed to be brilliant and productive, and you have had the support of parents, friends, local church, and the Christian community at large. The dreams they have for you are really big. So you left the land of your birth to migrate to a land of greener pastures and an opportunity to become a doctor. You were facilitated with a scholarship to accomplish this God-given prospect and most of all, the love of God was radiating in your heart so the road to success never looked so good.

There were many rude awakenings, which confronted you though when you got to the country where you were sent to study: the bright city lights, the pubs, entertainment centres, but your aim to achieve your goals could not be distracted by the overwhelming environment around you. You were fortunate to retain an 'A' level student, which was maintained for two consecutive years, then it started happening.

The decline suddenly began in the third year when you were invited out one night to celebrate and you just could not resist the urge to take a drink which later turned into drinks and the party turned into parties, your friends were no longer from the Christian council but they were from the social clubs at the university, who also encouraged smoking. The light of Jesus went out and the darkness came in. There was no longer time for prayer, Bible reading and church. Before you realized it, your life was spiraling downwards into sin and failure. The academics were pushed on the back burner, you lost control of the fight and the devil was winning the battle.

Thank God you still have a praying family and the church at home was seeking God and interceding constantly on your behalf. Prayer warriors prayed you back into the Kingdom of God. Praise God, the Holy Spirit convicted you when you almost reached your wit's end, just before you would have failed again and messed up your scholarship; the Lord heard the cry of the saints and took you back right on time. You are reading your Bible once more and the Holy Spirit has led you into the book of Daniel beginning at Chapter 1, where king Nebuchadnezzar of Babylon, besieged Israel and asked Asphenaz the master of his eunuchs to bring the children who had no blemish, but were well favoured, skilful in wisdom, cunning in knowledge and understanding science and who had the ability to stand in the king's palace, and learn the Chaldean language.

The Bible says, among them were the children of Judah, Daniel, Hananiah, Mishael, and Azariah: whom the prince of the eunuchs gave different names as follows: Belteshazzar, Shadrach, Meshach, and Abednego. The king appointed a daily portion of the king's meat and wine which he drank, as nourishment for three years, so that at the end they could appear before him. But Daniel purposed in his heart that he would not defile himself with the portion of the king's meat, neither with the wine which he drank. He asked the superintendent for permission to eat other things instead and God gave him special appreciation for Daniel and sympathy for his predicament.

"I am afraid you will become pale and thin compared with the other youths your age," he said, "and then the king will behead me for neglecting my responsibilities." Daniel suggested a trial of a ten-day diet of only vegetables and water. At the end of the ten days, Daniel and his friends looked healthier and better nourished than the youths who had been eating the food supplied by the king. As a result they were fed with vegetables and water without the rich food and wine.

God gave these four youths great ability to learn and they soon mastered all the literature and science of the time, and God gave Daniel the ability to understand the meanings of dreams and visions. When the three-year training period was completed, the superintendent brought all the young men to the king for oral exams, as he had been ordered to do. The King had long talks with each of them and none of them impressed him as much as these four young men. So they were put on his regular staff of advisors. And in all matters requiring information and balanced judgment, the king found these young men's advice ten times better than that of all the skilled magicians and wise astrologers in his realm. Daniel held the position as the king's counselor until the first year of the reign of King Cyrus.

Although Daniel was not living in the Jewish culture any longer but in the land of Babylon, he still decided that he would be faithful to the laws of the Jewish religion even before they faced the king's delicacies. They stuck to their conviction and God rewarded their faithfulness. Sometimes we get into trouble because we do not decide beforehand where to draw the line and we are persuaded and lured into situations that are unplanned. When we serve our God faithfully (as Daniel and his friends did) and maintain our allegiance to God we are rewarded with His promotions, favour and success, and we would be above our contemporaries.

We ought to let our lights shine for Jesus and to be the salt of the earth that our good deeds would be seen and in doing so we draw others to Jesus and praise the Father in heaven (Matthew 5:14-16). When we are not partakers of what the people of the world participate in, but take a stand for God, He will bless us with his favour, in health and better countenance. Paul said to Timothy, ***"Let no man despise thy youth, but be an example of the believers, in word, in conversation, in charity, in spirit, in faith, in purity…give attendance to reading, to exhortation, to doctrine"*** (1Timothy 4: 12&13 KJV). Paul was asking Timothy in spite of his youth, to set a standard in love etc. so that others could see Christ in him. Young people ought to do likewise and win their peers to the Lord.

If you have fallen victim to the prey of the enemy and fell out of grace, or even came short of what God was expecting of you, Jesus is waiting with arms open wide to bring you back to the place where you first began. Paul in writing to the Romans said, ***'I beseech you therefore brethren, by the mercies of God (I plead with you to give your bodies to God) that you present your bodies a living sacrifice, holy, acceptable (the kind he can accept) which is your reasonable service (when you think of what He has done for you, is this too much to ask?) And be not conformed to this world (don't copy the behaviour and customs***

of the world), but be transformed by the renewing of your mind (but be a new and different person with a fresh newness in all you do and think). That you may prove what is that good, and acceptable, perfect, will of God (then you will learn from your own experience how His ways will really satisfy you)' (Romans12: 1&2 KJV &TLB).

Don't let the world squeeze you into its mould, but be transformed in your mind and body by the indwelling power of God. The enemy would use your peers and friends to lure you into the pitfalls of the enemy so that when he gets you into his trap of sin you lose your focus and miss God's plan and vision for your life. God had a big plan for Daniel, Shadrach, Meshach and Abednego; but there were many trials they had to go through as strangers in a foreign and idolatrous land. Were they going to be conformed to the cultures, customs and worship of a different land or were they determined to stick to the God they knew was the true and living God? Let us check their lives out further and find out what else they went through.

Don't forget your dreams and visions

In Daniel chapter 2, Nebuchadnezzar had a terrifying nightmare, and awoke trembling with fear and he could not remember his dream! Immediately he called in all his magicians, incantationists, sorcerers, and astrologers, and demanded that they tell him what his dream had been.

The astrologers said to the king, "Sir, tell us the dream and then we can tell you what it means."

But the king replied, "I tell you, the dream is gone, I can't remember it. And if you won't tell me what it was and what it means, I'll have you torn limb from limb and your houses made into heaps of rubble! But I will give you many wonderful gifts and honours if you tell me what the dream was and what it means. So, begin!"

They said again, "How can we tell you what the dream means unless you tell us what it was?" … "There isn't a man alive who can tell others what they have dreamed! And there isn't a king in the world who would ask such a thing! This is an impossible thing the king requires, No one except the gods can tell you your dream and they are not here to help."

Upon hearing this, the king was furious, and sent out orders to execute all the wise men of Babylon. And Daniel and his companions were rounded up with the others to be killed. But when Ari-och, the chief executioner, came to kill them, Daniel handled the situation with great wisdom by asking, "Why is the king so angry? What is the matter?" Then Ari-och told him all that had happened.

So Daniel went in to see the king. "Give me a little time," he said, "and I will tell you the dream and what it means." Then he went home and told Hananiah, Mishael, and Azariah (their Jewish names), his companions. They asked the God of heaven to show them His mercy by telling them the secret, so they would not die with the others. That night in a vision God told Daniel what the king had dreamed.

Then Daniel praised the God of heaven saying, ***"Blessed be the name of God forever and ever, for He alone has all wisdom and all power. World events are ordered under His control. He removes kings and sets others on their thrones. He gives wise men their wisdom, and scholars their intelligence. He reveals profound mysteries beyond man's understanding. He knows all hidden things, for he is light, and darkness is no obstacle to Him. I thank and praise you, O God of my fathers, for you have given me wisdom and glowing health, and now, even this vision of the king's dream, and the understanding of what it means"*** (Daniel 2: 20-23 TBL).

Daniel went in to see Ari-och and said, "Don't kill them. Take me to the king and I will tell him what he wants to know." Daniel had faith and confidence in God knowing that He will hear his and his friends' prayers; once again he is proving the faithfulness of his God. Daniel reminded the king of his dream and gave him the interpretation. Daniel said "Thus the great God has shown what will happen in the future, and this interpretation of your dream is as sure and certain as my description of it."

"Truly, O Daniel," the king said, "your God is the God of gods, Ruler of kings, the Revealer of mysteries, because He has told you this secret."

Then the king made Daniel very great; he gave him many costly gifts, and appointed him to be ruler over the whole province of Babylon, as well as chief over all his wise men. Then Daniel requested that the king appoint Shadrach, Meshach and Abednego (Babylonian names) as Daniel's assistants, to be in charge of all the affairs of the province of Babylon; Daniel served as chief magistrate in the king's court.

When you are going through your moment of crisis, do not panic but persist in prayer. Panic confirms your hopelessness; prayer confirms your hope in God. Daniel's trust in God saved his life, his three friends' and the lives of the other people. He took time to give God praise for revealing the dream and vision and credit Him for all wisdom and power. Sometimes we forget to be thankful to God for answering our prayers and for the revelation of his understanding and wisdom. Daniel and his friends were also rewarded with gifts, positions and promotions, these are God's favours. Wait for your promotion from God, it may come when you least expect it, just keep on being faithful.

Have you forgotten or lost your dream that God has given you? Your dreams and visions can be obscured by focusing on the wrong things or the trouble that you are facing. Job says ***"God has blocked my path and turned my light to darkness. He has***

stripped me of my glory and removed the crown from my head. He has broken me down on every side, and I am done for. He has destroyed all hope. His fury burns against me; he counts me as an enemy." Job's wife did not stand with him in his trials neither did his friends who came to be with him; he was alone except for God. That was only for a time, when God was ready to bless Job he gave him a double portion.

Edward Moore wrote a song, 'When darkness seems to hide His face, I rest on His unchanging grace. When all around my soul gives way, He then is all my hope and stay. On Christ the solid Rock I stand, all other ground is sinking sand; all other ground is sinking sand'. Don't go under your circumstances and lose your dreams and visions, seek God even if you don't have others agreeing with you. God will give you a revelation of what He has in store for you. It is so easy to lose sight when the light suddenly turns into darkness but it is in these times that God develops your night vision.

It may be that you are in a foreign country and you need finance to continue your studies. You cannot get funding to continue your studies, or you can't get a job; maybe when you get one you are underpaid. You can't pay your bills or you can hardly eat a proper meal; you live on biscuits and milk for your sustenance. It is difficult to find somewhere to stay, difficult to concentrate on your studies because there is so much pressing in on you and it seems as though there is no way out.

Do not lose your focus and turn to other things that will cause you to lose your salvation. Pray and watch God turn your situation around in your favour. ***'For thou, Lord, will bless the righteous with favour and compass him with a shield'*** (Psalm5:12 NKJV). God wants to test your faithfulness so He is trying you to see what your responses are going to be. Pray and ask God for solutions and revelation. He will be faithful and come to your rescue and fulfill your dreams.

In Daniel chapter 3, the king made an image of gold whose height was three score cubits and the breath was six cubits and set it up in the plain of Duca, in the province of Babylon. He then sent messengers to all the princes, governors, captains, judges, treasurers, counselors, sheriffs, and rulers of all the provinces of his empire, to come to the dedication of his statue. When they came and stood before the monument, a herald shouted out, "O people of all nations and languages, this is the king's command: When the band strikes up, you are to fall flat on the ground to worship King Nebuchadnezzar's golden statue; anyone who refuses to obey will immediately be thrown into a flaming furnace." So when the band began to play, everyone present, regardless to his nation, language, or religion was to fall on the ground and worship the statue. But some officials went to the king and accused some of the Jews of refusing to worship!

They said "Some Jews out there – Shadrach, Meshach and Abednego, whom you have put in charge of Babylonian affairs, have defied you, refusing to serve your gods or to worship the golden statue you set up." Then Nebuchadnezzar, in a terrible rage, ordered these young men to be brought in before him. He asked if it was true that they refused to worship his statue and offered them one more chance when the music played that they will bow and worship the statue or if not they would be thrown into a flaming furnace within the hour. He asked, "What god can deliver you out of my hands?"

Shadrach, Meshach and Abednego replied, "O Nebuchadnezzar, we are not worried about what will happen to us. If we are thrown into the flaming furnace, our God is able to deliver us; and he will deliver us out of your hand, Your Majesty. But if he doesn't, please understand, sir, that even then we will never under any circumstance serve your gods or worship the golden statue you have erected."

Then Nebuchadnezzar was filled with fury and his face became dark with anger at them. He commanded that the furnace be heated up seven times hotter than usual, and called for some of the strongest men of his army to bind Shadrach, Meshach and Abednego, and throw them into the fire. So they bound them tight with ropes and threw them into the furnace, fully clothed. The king demanded such a hot fire in the furnace, the flames leaped out and killed the soldiers as they threw them in!

Suddenly, as he was watching, Nebuchadnezzar jumped up in amazement and exclaimed to his advisors, "Didn't we throw three men into the furnace? Well, look! I see four men, unbound, walking around in the fire, and they aren't even hurt by the flames! And the fourth looks like the Son of God." He went as close as he could to the open door of the flaming furnace and yelled: "Shadrach, Meshach and Abednego, servants of the Most High God! Come out! Come here!" So they stepped out of the fire.

Then all the people gathered around them; not a hair on their heads was singed; their coats were un-scorched, and they didn't even smell of smoke! Then Nebuchadnezzar said, "Blessed be the God of Shadrach, Meshach and Abednego, for he sent his angel to deliver his trusting servants when they defied the king's commandment, and were willing to die rather than serve or worship any god except their own. Therefore, I make this decree, that any person of any nation, language, or religion who speaks a word against the God of Shadrach, Meshach and Abednego, shall be torn limb by limb and his house knocked into a heap of rubble. For no other God can do what this one does."

Have you been caught in a fire of adversity, temptation, trial, dispute, and despondency, what ever it is? You can come through it like the Hebrew boys as long as Jesus is in the fire with you. ***'These trials are only to test your faith, to see whether or not it is strong and pure. It is being tested as fire tests gold and purifies it; and yours is far more precious to God than mere gold; so if your faith remains strong after being tried in the test tube of fiery trials, it will bring you much praise and glory and honour on the day of His return'*** (1Peter 1:7 TLB). Do not bow to the things that are presented to you for worship that take the place of God. They may be material things such as your car, house, money, clothes; even your friend or friends can stand in the way of God. They may be essentials but do not give them priority in your life over God.

God is counting on you to be as one of the Hebrew boys. They were unswerving. They had already made up their mind they were not bowing to any image. This was yet another trial for them but they had decided whether God delivered them or not they were not going to bow. Is someone trying to make you surrender to a situation in which you know you should not succumb to, but the person is applying pressure and he/she is not giving up? It may be a relationship that has developed and become too close for comfort. You are asked to do something that is against the will of God. Remember, you are His child and He has a perfect plan for your life, don't do anything to jeopardize your destiny.

When you stand for godly principles, the world may not understand or appreciate you but you still need to take a stand because it is by the manifestations of your fruits that you can win the lost. Nebuchadnezzar told the men to light the furnace seven times hotter; seven is a number of completion. The heat may be turned on at its hottest temperature, but God knows how much you can bear and He knows when your fiery trial should finish. When Nebuchadnezzar saw the power of God in operation as the men walked up and down in the fire and the form of the son of God as the fourth man in the fire, he had to bless the God of these Hebrew boys and made a proclamation and a declaration.

You may be bound by situations and circumstances in life but you are not alone, Jesus Christ is in the fire with you. The fire only destroyed the ropes but it did not hurt the Hebrew boys. Your trial is not meant to hurt you but to make you strong and to bring you out victorious, so walk up and down or dance in your fire because Jesus is with you. God will bring you out victoriously and vindicate you for His righteousness, just hang in there a little longer until He brings you out.

Others are observing and are looking to see how you are getting along and how you would come out. When you do come out they would want to know how you made it through. Then you will have a testimony telling of God's goodness. You will tell them it was because of His mercy, love, faithfulness, divine intervention, why you made it. It was not because of man's theology, theory, and evidence, they could not suffice to bring you through a fire: it was God and Jesus Christ divine intervention and the power of the Holy Ghost, which had the capacity and ability to bring you through.

As your critics dare you to pass the test they have set before you, wishing you will never win, as they gang up on you and tell tales on you, planning your demise and failure, they feel that there is no way you can win or pass this test. Who do you believe in and put your confidence in? Are you going to prove them true or wrong? Are you willing to show them that God is a faithful and true God and He will never disappoint you? Do not settle for sub-standards in life, hold to the principle of God, and discipline your mind so that you will not flunk in your quest of serving God. God has it all worked out for you to be a winner and not a loser. The Hebrews boys knew what their beliefs were, now it was God's time to show His mighty acts.

Are there folks in your life who hate you because God saw it fit to bless you, favour and promote you due to your faithfulness to Him? You may have people on your job who undermine you at times, carrying news or gossip on you, or trying to use satanic means to have you removed from your position. You may be even experiencing a tough time at school with your peers who would try anything to hurt you, whether it is physically or otherwise, trying to seduce into evil practices. The works of the enemy cannot prevail over the lives of the children of God, for no weapons form against you shall prosper. It may seem as though they are prospering but that is only for a season, the children of God shall triumph in due course of time.

After the reign of Nebuchadnezzar, there was Belshazzar, the Chaldean king. When he was killed, Darius reigned in his stead. King Darius divided the kingdom into provinces, each under a governor. In Daniel 6 the governors were accountable to three presidents (Daniel was the first of them) so that the king could administer the kingdom efficiently. Daniel soon proved himself more capable than all the other presidents and governors, for he had great ability, and the king began to think of placing him over the entire empire as his administrative officer. This made the other presidents and governors very jealous and they began searching for some fault in the way Daniel was handing his affairs so that they could complain to the king about him. But they couldn't find anything to criticize! He was faithful and honest, and made no mistakes, so they concluded, "Our only chance is his religion!"

They decided to go to the king and say, "King Darius, live forever! We presidents, governors, counselors and deputies have unanimously decided that you should make a law, irrevocable under any circumstance, that for the next thirty days anyone who asks a favour of God or man except from you, Your Majesty, shall be thrown to the lions. Your Majesty, we request your signature on this law; sign it so that it cannot be canceled or changed. It will be a 'law of the Medes and Persians' that cannot be revoked." So the king signed the law.

But though Daniel knew about it, he went home and knelt down as usual in his upstairs bedroom, with its windows open toward Jerusalem, and prayed three times a day, just as he always had, giving thanks to his God. Then the men thronged to Daniel's house and found him praying there, asking favours of his God. They rushed back to the king and reminded him about his law. "Haven't you signed a decree," they said, "that permits no petitions to any God or man, except you, for thirty days? And anyone disobeying will be thrown to the lions?" "Yes," the king replied, "it is 'a law of the Medes and Persians,' that cannot be altered or revoked."

Daniel was resolute in his mind and very persuaded that no one was going to prevent him from praying even though a decree was signed. He had proven God's faithfulness through his special diet, he proved Him in revealing dreams and interpretations, and he knew that God delivered Shadrach, Meshach and Abednego, from the fiery furnace, so why would He not deliver him now from the mouths of the lions? Do not let what your colleagues say hinder you from praying, we need to start showing off the mighty God we are serving and how He can come through with mighty acts on our behalf.

Then they told the king, "That fellow Daniel, one of the Jewish captives, is paying no attention to you or your law. He is asking favour of His God three times a day." The King became very angry with himself for signing the law, and determined to save Daniel. He spent the rest of the day trying to think of some way to get Daniel out of this predicament. In the evening the men came again to the king and said, "Your Majesty, there is nothing you can do. You signed the law and it cannot be changed."

So at last the king gave the order for Daniel's arrest, and he was taken to the den of lions. The king said to him, "May your God, whom you worship continually deliver you." And then they threw him in. A stone was brought and placed over the mouth of the den; and the king sealed it with his own signet ring, and that of his government, so that no one could rescue Daniel from the lions. Then the king returned to his palace and went to bed without dinner. He refused his usual entertainment and didn't sleep all night. Very early the next morning he hurried out to the lion's den, and called out in anguish, "O Daniel, servant of the Living God, was your God, whom you worship continually, able to deliver you from the lions?"

Then he heard a voice! "Your Majesty, live forever!" It was Daniel! "My God sent his angel," he said, "to shut the lions' mouths so that they couldn't touch me; for I am innocent before God, nor, sir, have I wronged you." The king was beside himself with joy and ordered that Daniel be lifted from the den. And not a scratch was found on him, because he believed in His God.

Then the king issued a command to bring the men who had accused Daniel, and throw them into the den along with their children and wives, and the lions leaped upon them and tore them apart before they even hit the bottom of the den. Afterwards, King Darius wrote this message addressed to everyone in his empire:

"Greetings! I decree that everyone shall tremble and fear before the God of Daniel in every part of my kingdom. For His God is the living, unchanging God whose kingdom shall never end. He delivers His people, preserving them from harm; he does great miracles in heaven and earth; it is He who delivered Daniel from the power of the lions." So Daniel prospered in the reign of Darius and in the reign of Cyrus the Persian.

Satan would **pounce** on you at some time in your life, but know for sure that there is a **price** to **pay** in order for you to gain a **prize**. Daniel was determined in his mind that he was going to prove that his God was the one and only true, living and powerful God and God was there supporting him through all of his trials to bring him through victoriously in every one of these tests. The different kings at the end of each test were now able to make a new proclamation and decree because of the stand that Daniel and his friends took. They were a great team; they were promoted from a hard place to a high place in the land of Babylon. This is God's principle for them and for us as well. When you 'purpose in your heart' to honour God, He blesses you and becomes involved in your life in ways you never thought possible.

When your enemy is determined to see your demise, you have to be persistent likewise. Use the weapon of prayer and overcome his resistance. He may be out to get your life but God has a bigger plan and would defeat him by all means. ***'You have to keep on doing God's will if you want him to do for you all that He has promised'*** (Hebrews 10: 36 TLB). The governors and presidents, deputies and counselors were busy making mischief in the courts of Babylon laying snares for Daniel and his friends, but God's plan was at the end of the season His name would be established as the Lord of the Most High and He would be the true and living God that this idolatrous nation shall turn to and worship.

God is looking for men and women today like Daniel, Shadrach, Meshach and Abednego, who are willing to change, challenge and break traditions of men; which are not synchronized with the Word of God. His will or plan will come forth, so that men's heart will be turned to God. God needs people who will be visionary and give birth to institutions, programs and organizations, to lift the cause of Christ by helping the needy, down-trodden, poverty stricken, drug-addicted, forsaken, lonely,

HIV AIDS victim; to advance the kingdom of Jesus Christ. When He finds these people He uses them to unlock doors and new dimensions of His power to bring grace, hope, new life, restored health and healing; to fulfill God's will and purpose for peoples' lives.

As God's redeemed people you are loved, valued and protected, so stand on that truth. You may have to endure hardship for your faith or fight to survive in a foreign land. Understand this, that God will let the devil know, He has too much invested in you already to let you be destroyed. There have been enough trials, hardships, training and discipline, so he has to take his filthy hands off you because you belong to the Most High God. Rejoice! God is protecting you.

Chapter 10

'GO FOR IT'

We can safely say that the keys to a successful life is knowing what you are called to do and who you are and what are your skills, gifts and talents. Another key is having the spiritual and emotional energy and passion to get you there. When you find out what is your God-given purpose, you will always have a passion with it, so 'go for it'.

A passion is what will keep your dream alive even when the flames are burning low and you have to fan the fire, or pour the anointing of the Holy Spirit on it to keep it burning. This passion keeps you up at nights when everyone else has gone to bed. It pulsates, puts you on a high when everyone else is on a low and they are wondering what is wrong with you. It makes you see things when everyone else's vision is blurred. It makes you want to go after your dream with a vicious tenacity. Everything around you may look dark and dismal but you are ready to take it by force: ***'... the kingdom of heaven suffers violence, and the violent men take it by force'*** (Matthew11:12 NAS).

A passionate person with a limited ability will out-perform a person with much greater ability. Why? Because there is an inner spirit that propels you beyond your human comprehension and compassion, because passionate people have zeal and enthusiasm to aspire and achieve their goals in life. If you are passionate about the dream and vision that God has for you then 'go for it' with all your might; regardless of how tired you are, how many people tried and failed, and how they may speak ill of you, you can do it, so 'go for it'.

There are some things you may need to put in place, like: prayer, coming up with a plan, studying it, analyzing, coming up with methods, but 'go for it' regardless to who wants to talk you out of it or criticize you. It may not be perfect the first time but try and try until you come up with the right solution, or what you are looking for. Let you passion spur you on.

A passionate person would rather live with the pain of risk and the comfort of knowing that they tried than to regret that they never made any effort at all. Even though other people may think that you are too old to try certain things and you know that age is just a number and age does not matter to you, let them say what they want but you 'go for it.' God would honour you for your passion. The psalmist is encouraging us when he says (Psm.138:8TLB) ***'The Lord will work out His plans for my life – for your loving kindness, Lord, continues forever. Don't abandon me, for you made me'.***

The story is told of an old donkey, which had served his master well on the farm. The master had planned to get rid of him but each time he tried; he often found some way of keeping him because he was still quite helpful around the farm.

The farmer was doing some construction so there was this large hole somewhere around the farm yard and accidentally one day the old donkey happened to fall in it. The farmer was very distraught and felt sorry for him. Tried as he may, by all efforts on his own he could not get the donkey out so he decided to get some help from his neighbours. They came and looked at the situation and tried to assist the farmer but they too could not help. The only solution they could come up with, was for the farmer to bury the donkey seeing that he was already in the hole. So they started throwing sand on him, while he was lying down in the hole.

The donkey felt the heavy loads of sand being thrown on him. The donkey thought to himself 'Why must these people throw sand on me, I am not dead'. With that realization he got up from where he was. He felt that he should not only shake the sand from off his body but there was need to shake the sand from around his feet and to step up on it. So he started the process of shaking off and stepping up, shaking off and stepping up. Each time the sand was thrown on him, he was shaking off and stepping up until he came to the top of the hole, where he just stepped out of what was once a hole. You can imagine how surprised everyone was to see that the old donkey used his brain and improvised a master plan that these people did not even think was possible.

The moral behind this story is that people can write you off, term you as expired and finished with, but it is your duty and decision to rise above the verdict of your critics. You have to believe the report and plan of the Lord, and tell them that the Lord is not finished with you as yet. You are still fighting and there are still more battles to be fought, seas to cross, victories to win, armies to conquer and you are on the winning side because Jesus is on your side and it's not over until God says it's over. There is no storm that He has brought you to that He can't bring you through, if even He has to come walking on those rough seas to get you. He will, so 'go for it.'

Going after your dreams may mean completing your education, or maybe getting a Degree, completing the project you started years ago, going for the training to acquire the skill you always thought you would like to have. Maybe now that the children are grown and have left home, it is time that you take the holiday trip you had planned to take fifteen years ago, or the business venture you had been so indecisive about. Maybe it's time, 'go for it.' What about the dream home you planned to buy so long ago? You keep changing locations. Why don't you make it a matter of prayer and let God direct you according to his will. ***'The steps of a good man are ordered by the Lord'*** (Psm.37:23).

Whatever path you have chosen, stay focused and prioritize your goals. Give it some serious thoughts and time. You can be distracted easily if you have too many things doing at one time. It would cause confusion in your life. You would be wondering, 'what it is again that I have to do today?' One thing at a time and it would be done better than a lot of things at one time. Get rid of the clutter in your life, keep it simple but great. You know what it is to work in a cluttered kitchen; having a cluttered handbag or cluttered clothes closet, keeping a cluttered desk. It is havoc, isn't it? You can't find things when you want them. So it is with a cluttered or clustered life.

If your priorities are not aligned with passion, start making some adjustments, it will do you a lot of good. Jeremiah said, ***'O Lord, I know it is not within the power of a man to map his life and plan his course – so you correct me, Lord; but please be gentle. Don't do it in your anger, for I would die'*** (Jeremiah10: 23, 24TLB). Let God control your destiny, so that He can control the outcome. You may have outgrown your boundaries and are still hanging on to the things that have become so familiar to you and you are afraid to get out of your comfort zone. You are afraid of risks. God may be beckoning you to get into bigger things but you are afraid that you do not have the skill or ability to deal with a bigger project. With it comes bigger problems, distress and stress, so you remain in the box where it is safer to operate.

What you don't realize is that God wants you to move on, especially if He has earmarked you for a particular purpose, like taking care of the poor, protecting the rights of the under-privileged, enforcing the law, defending the abused or the molested. Don't flinch from your responsibility with the excuse that someone else will do it. God has given you a voice, so speak up, He has given you a platform, so stand up. He will dry up your brook where you are, like Elijah, so that you will have to move on. So, 'go for it'.

What might have worked for you yesterday might not work for you today. God will show you the signs for you to move on. Galatians 6: 5 says ***'Each one should carry his own load.'*** That is why He gives you the zeal to bring you into the fulfillment of His plan for your life, so 'go for it'. He is waiting for you to say yes, so that He can open the door of opportunity for you to walk into. God is saying, ***'I will instruct you and teach you in the***

way you should go; I will counsel you and watch over you' (Psalm 32:8 NIV).

Hard work brings success

When your dreams become a reality, they can be successful, just be consistent and keep at it. If you have a dream about writing a book, start writing, don't start with looking for a publisher. That would come in time. You don't have to be great at first but you have to start in order to be great. It can also be a gradual process. One word of caution, don't go about telling everybody your dream, because the enemy is a deceiver. Beware of his cunning devices; he knows how to set up road blocks. He would send the wrong people in your life and before you know it, they would talk you out of it or distract you. If you are not strong enough, before you know it your dream is aborted.

If you are lazy and do not like to work hard you might not make it also. God is looking at your attitude, you have to be militant, not sleeping when you should be working, or looking at television when you should be studying. You need to have a disciplined mind, one that is willing to work. You have to be organized also, not turning up to do a lecture and you forgot your notes, or turning up for an exam half an hour late. Or, you can't expect God to help you to pass your exams if you don't study, unless you are a genius. God expects you to do your part and to be responsible. You don't appear before an honourable person in shabby clothes, you want to be immaculately dressed. You just don't do things anyhow, in any old way and expect God to bless you; you must be prepared and be vigilant at all times.

A story was often related in the Caribbean about a lady who went to the river to wash her clothes and would make it in record time. Her neighbour always observed her and wondered how she made it so soon and her clothes were always sparkling bright when she hung them out. She decided to ask her the secret. The lady told her that the Lord helped her each time with her washing. Well, this other lady decided that she was going to take her clothes to the river and ask the Lord to help her too. She went to the river the next day and put her clothes on a stone in the river and sat on another stone and kept on saying, "Lord help me wash these clothes", from morning until evening. She finally picked up her bundle and left for home with her clothes still not washed. The saying goes: "The Lord help those who help themselves". Don't expect God to do the job all by Himself.

In Nehemiah's day the people had a mind to work. He was in Shushan the palace, when he got the report from men of Judah who had escaped, that the remnant of the captivity were in great affliction and reproach. The wall of Jerusalem also was broken down, and the gates were burned with fire (Nehemiah 1:2-3). When Nehemiah heard these things he sat down and wept; mourned certain days, fasted and prayed before God. As he served the king Artaxerxes his wine, the king noticed he was sad and he told the king the reason. The king asked what could be done. Before Nehemiah replied, he made a quick prayer to God.

Nehemiah replied, "If it please Your Majesty and if you look upon me with your royal favour, send me to Judah to rebuild the city of my fathers!"

The king replied, with the queen sitting beside him, "How long will you be gone? When will you return?" Nehemiah set a time and it was agreed! And he set a time for his departure. Then he added this to his request: "If it please the king, give me letters to the governors west of the Euphrates River instructing them to let me travel through their countries on my way to Judah; also a letter to Asaph, the manager of the king's forest, instructing him to give me timber for the beams and for the gates of the fortress near the Temple, and for the city walls, and for a house for myself." And the king granted these requests; for God was being gracious to him; (Nehemiah was an organized person, he planned well).

Nehemiah had opposition; Samballat, who was very angry when he learned that they were rebuilding the wall. He flew into a rage, insulted and mocked and laughed at Nehemiah and the Jews. He did so with his friends and the Samaritan army officers. "What does this bunch of poor feeble Jews think they are doing? He scoffed. "Do they think they can build the wall in a day if they offer enough sacrifices? And look at those charred stones they are pulling out of the rubbish and using again!" Tobiah, who was standing beside him remarked, "If even a fox walked along the top of their wall, it would collapse!"

Then Nehemiah prayed, ***"Hear us, O Lord God, for we are being mocked. May their scoffing fall back upon their own heads, and may they themselves become captives in a foreign land! Do not ignore their sin. Do not blot it out, for they have despised You, in despising us who are building your wall."*** Nehemiah prayed about everything, he did not take things into his own hand, but also made a request for God to handle his enemies and what he must do with them. God will take care of your enemies, let them go ahead and deride and mock you.

The wall was finished in early September, just fifty-two days after they had begun. When their enemies and surrounding nations heard about it, they were frightened and humiliated, and they realized that the work had been done with the help of God. Although they worked hard amidst the opposition, God got the glory out of what was accomplished.

There are some lessons here to be learnt; you can't be lazy and accomplish anything. Nehemiah's heart was in the right place, in that he was moved by compassion for what was taking place. He believed that he could make a difference, he was strategically placed in the king's palace, serving the king's wine so that he could have the king's favour. He had most of the people's support and most of all they had a mind to work. You can have the King's favour; just start serving Him. 'Then you will win favour and a good name in the sight of God and man' (Proverbs 3:4 NIV).

Think wisely and clearly

You cannot just stumble into good prospects if you don't keep a good head and think your way through clearly. The Proverbs say, as a man thinks in his heart that is who he is (Proverbs 23:7). You have to think sober thoughts, no matter what the calling on your life is. Your level of success would increase as your thoughts are positive, as you think out of the box and extend your vision. In other words; the wider the spectrum of your thoughts are, the wider your prospects for success will be.

James 1:5&6 (TLB) says ***'If you want to know what God wants you to do, ask Him, and He will gladly tell you. He is always ready to give a bountiful supply of wisdom to all who ask Him, He will not resent it.'*** If in your asking God and you are doubtful that He will give it to you, then you are not expecting that the Lord would give you an answer. A doubtful mind will be unsettled as a wave of the sea that is driven and tossed by the wind, and every decision you make will be uncertain, as you turn to this way and to that. You need guidance from God. The mind is a powerful instrument but you have to train it to 'think on things that are lovely, just and of a good report.' Also think ahead so that you can plan ahead and do not develop an ad hoc way of doing things, always have a back up system just in case one plan fails. This also helps to sharpen your reflexes.

You ought to have sharp reflexes to get out of difficulties easily. For example, when you find yourself in financial difficulty, what do you do to make some quick finances for a livelihood, or acquire other job skills? When you do not have these qualities you find it difficult to manage time, skill and finance. God wants us to be wise thinkers, so 'go for it'. The Proverbs say, 'If a man lacks wisdom, ask and He will give you liberally. The wise man looks ahead. The fool attempts to fool himself and won't face facts'. 'A wise man is cautious and avoids danger; a fool plunges ahead with great confidence' (Proverbs 14:8 &16).

The story is told of four leprous men in 2 Kings: 7 (TLB). There was famine in the land of Samaria and Elisha prophesied, "The Lord says that by this time tomorrow two gallons of flour or four gallons of barley grain will be sold in the markets of Samaria for a dollar!" The officer assisting the king said, "That couldn't happen if the Lord made windows in the sky!"

But Elisha replied, "You will see it happen, but you won't be able to buy any of it!" Now there were four lepers sitting outside the city gates. "Why sit here until we die?" they asked each other. "We will starve if we go back into the city; so we might as well go out and surrender to the Syrian army. If they let us live, so much the better; but if they kill us, we would have died anyway." They were thinking or reasoning among themselves, they were also using some wisdom and God was about to explore this and honour their reasoning and faith and bring a prophetic word to pass through these leprous men who were despised.

So that evening they went out to the camp of the Syrians but there was no one there! For the Lord had made the whole Syrian army hear the clatter of speeding chariots and a loud galloping of horses and the sounds of a great army approaching. "The King of Israel has hired the Hittites and Egyptians to attack us" they cried out. So they panicked and fled into the night, abandoning their tents, horses, donkeys, and everything else. This was a set up by God.

When the lepers arrived at the edge of the camp they went into one tent after another, eating, drinking wine, and carrying out silver and gold and clothing and hiding it. Finally, they said to each other, "This isn't right. This is wonderful news, and we aren't sharing it with anyone! If we wait until morning, some terrible calamity will certainly fall upon us; come on, let's go back and tell the people at the palace." Here is wisdom again; they were ready to share the good news.

So they went back to the city and told the watchmen what had happened. The watchmen shouted the news to those in the palace. The king got out of bed and told his officers, I know what has happened. The Syrians know we are starving, so they have left their camp and have hidden in the fields, thinking that we will be lured out of the city. Then they will attack us and get in and make slaves of us."

Four chariot-horses were found and the king sent out two charioteers to see where the Syrians had gone. They followed a trail of clothing and equipment all the way to the Jordon River, thrown away by the Syrians in their haste. The scouts returned and told the king, and the people of Samaria rushed out and plundered the camp of the Syrians. So it was true that two gallons of flour and four gallons of barley were sold that day for one dollar, just as the Lord had said! The king appointed his special assistant to control the traffic at the gate, but he was knocked down, trampled and killed as the people rushed out (the same officer who said it could not happen, so Elisha's prophesy came to pass).

If you have adopted the habit of thinking wisely and clearly and have trained your mind to have the mind of God; He would one day cause the ungodly businessman to be distracted by a heavenly noise and he would run from the location and that business that you have been thinking about and planning for all these months and years is going to fall right in your hand. That scholarship that was to have gone to someone, God is about to let something happen and the person is about to change their mind and you are going to take his place because God sees that you work hard and you deserve it. Whatever you are thinking, as long as it is wise thinking, God can make it happen for you, so train your mind to think positively.

You may be thinking that it is not fair when some people are prospering or they are being more successful than others. It is God's favour upon their lives. Thinking positively can be a new way to your success. Discipline your mind and always remember to pray. Don't forget the four lepers did not hoard all for themselves. They felt if they just continue to hide everything for themselves they could get into trouble, so they decided to share the good tidings. When God has opened a door and blessed you, you need to share with others. Don't forget to be grateful to God; give Him His portion first.

God can turn things around

In 2Kings: 8 there is Gehazi in the company of the king telling him about some great stories of the wonderful things Elisha did, about how he had brought back a boy to life. At that moment, the mother of the boy walked in. Elisha had told her to leave Samaria during the time of the famine. She has returned now that the famine is over, and is requesting her house and land from the king. The king is finding out from her if it is true what Gehazi was saying. She confirms that it is true, so the king directed that everything must be restored to her plus the value of the crops that had been harvested during her absence.

God looks out and looks after His people during the difficult times and He also restores what is rightfully yours, even though you were not in place to reap it and someone else reaped your harvest. It shall be yours; you would not have to start from scratch.

The question is, what is Gehazi doing in the presence of the king? He was struck with leprosy. It started when Naaman offered Elisha gifts after he was healed and Elisha refused them. Gehazi went after Naaman, giving him a false report and received two expensive robes and two bags of money supposedly to take to Elisha. Gehazi took the gifts from Naaman's servants and hid them in his house. Gehazi went back to Elisha, who asked him where he went. He replied that he did not go anywhere.

Elisha said to him, "Don't you realize that I was there in thought when Naaman stepped down from his chariot to meet you? Is this the time to receive money and clothing and olive farms and vineyards and sheep and oxen and servants? Because you have done this, Naaman's leprosy shall be upon you and upon your children and your children's children forever." Gehazi walked away from the room a leper, his skin as white as snow (2King 5:14-27).

Theologians believed it was Naaman and his sons who were the four leprous men. These four men could have received their healing on the way to spreading the good news. We are reminded of the story where Jesus told the leprous men to go and show themselves to the priest. While they were on the way they received their healing. Gehazi had a lot of reflection while he sat at the gate of Samaria and thought of where he went wrong. Having spent time with Elisha as his servant he knew and saw the power of God in operation, hence he would have spent some time in prayer and repentance and asked God's forgiveness.

When he saw all the silver, gold, clothes and food in the camp of the Syrians, Gehazi knew that it was not just a time of running and hiding all for themselves but they had to share the goods with the people of Samaria. The past experience changed his life. They helped to save thousands of lives in the nation and the prophetic word was fulfilled through these leprous men. The message brought him right into the presence of the king and made him a person of influence because the king is listening to him and is ready to take advice from him. Elisha had said to him that it was not the right time to receive gifts, but at this time, God's appointed time, he had received gifts and God's favour.

Greed sometimes gets us into trouble and cause unplanned dilemmas but thank God for His loving kindness and forgiveness, also His grace and mercy. You may have made some mistakes along the way but just repent, Jesus has already paid the price for your sins. Make amends and show God some evidence of change, and He will restore you, not just to your former state but He will give you gifts and His favour. He can reverse the damages and curses of your past and bring you into fulfillment for the future. Don't love yourself only but love others so that you will share what God has blessed you with and your life will have a positive impact on them.

God is also a God of restoration. He said ***"I will restore to you the years that the locusts have eaten, the cankerworm, and the caterpillar, and the palmerworm, my great army which I sent among you. And you shall eat in plenty and be satisfied, and praise the name of the Lord your God, who has dealt wondrously with you: and my people shall never be ashamed."*** (Joel2: 25 & 26). God will turn your life around that you will sit in the company of people with influence and affluence. You cannot begin to imagine what God will do.

Have you noticed how these men had a team spirit, they were saying the same thing. If you find it difficult to work by yourself get someone who will co-operate with you, one who would understand and come in agreement with you. ***'…if any two of you shall agree on earth as touching anything that they shall ask, it shall be done of you of my Father who is in heaven'*** (Matthew 18:19 KJV). Get a mentor, or one who would give you the nudge or the push you need to make that move. You've probably been sitting for too long. Don't sit until you die, or until you can't move and you are handicapped. Get up, change your position. Get cracking and 'go for it'.

Notice they did not say, 'We have leprosy so let us sit here and wait, in any case we will die, there is no chance of coming out of this.' No, they challenged themselves. It is not your time to wait on death to strike, so don't quit because of discouragement or lack of finance and motivation, be a person of action, whatever you have started, you can complete. You can do all things through Christ who strengthens you and begin a good work within you. He is able to bring it to perfection. Responsible people follow through regardless to negative or positive evaluators.

The crisis that you have experienced may have caused you to fall and have a terrible spell. It can be a disguise for your future blessing, or can be used to lift you to a greater dimension far above where you were previously. But you need to pull yourself up by your boot straps, dust yourself off, and tell yourself that you have to make a move and you will make it, because you have been sitting too long now. You may not have someone to confer with you, but all you need is to ask God for the strength to do it and he will give you the desire of your heart, so 'Go for it'.

Chapter 11

BETTER NOT BITTER

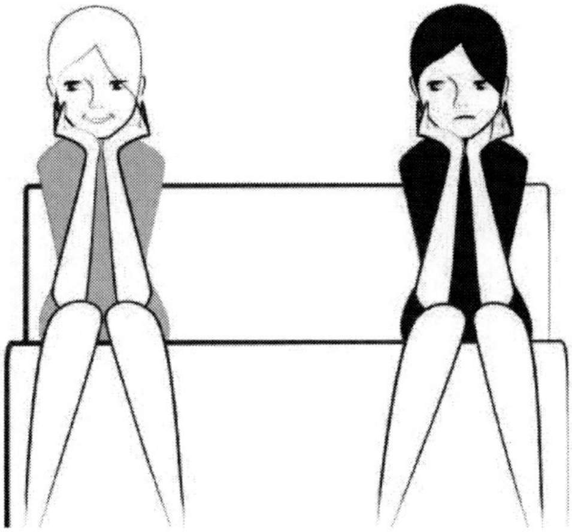

Did you have some tough times in your life and you are bitter about it? You said you will never forget those who hurt you; they are there in your chest (emotionally) like an ulcer eating it out. You can't sleep, you are not eating properly, you are feeling sick and when you visit the doctor, he does not know what is wrong with you. The person you are hurting is yourself, because the one who has hurt you has moved on with their life and you are stuck in the mud with your wheels broken off; like the Egyptians when they were chasing after the Israelites.

Get rid of the hurt before it kills you. The reason why God allowed it was simply to qualify you for where He is about to take you. What you are doing is to take it out on God because you stopped serving Him. You say a loving God could not stand by and see people hurt you like that and do nothing. God saw what was being done to His son but He had to look away when

His son was cruelly crucified on the cross as He took on the sins of the whole world. He could not look on sin. Jesus said, ***"Father forgive them; they do not know what they are doing"*** (Luke 23:34KJV). Jesus set an example by forgiving so we have to forgive also. Who are we not to go through some ills in life? Without the cross there is no crown, so don't stay bitter, because you will not be able to go where God is taking you with bitterness in your heart. Let us look at the life of Naomi as our reference.

Ruth holds fast to Naomi for a better not a bitter future

In the Book of Ruth it is recorded that Naomi left Jerusalem for Moab with her husband and two sons because of famine. Her husband, Elimelech, died and her sons, Mahlon and Chilion, married Orpah and Ruth, but later both men died also, so that Naomi was left alone without her husband and her sons. Later, Naomi decided that she was going back to Israel with her daughters-in-law for she heard that the famine had gone. Some time on the journey she changed her mind and entreated them to return to their parents. She told them, "May the Lord reward you for your faithfulness to your husbands and to me. And may He bless you with another happy marriage." Then she kissed them and they all broke down and cried.

Orpah and Ruth insisted that they wanted to go but Naomi told them it was better for them to return to their own people. She told them "… Oh how I grieve for you that the Lord has punished me in a way that injures you." And again they cried together, Orpah kissed her mother-in-law goodbye, and returned to her childhood home. It was ordained by God that Orpah would leave; it was also in the mind of God that Naomi should stop and change her mind. There are some people who God will allow to leave you, while others will stay as long as He is controlling your destiny; He has the final say.

Ruth replied, "Don't make me leave you, for I want to go wherever you go, and to live wherever you live. Your people shall be my people, and your God shall be my God. I want to die where you die, and be buried there. May the Lord do terrible things to me if I allow anything but death to separate us." That is what you call commitment, loyalty and love. She turned her back on the past and was about to face a new future, leaving her country and an idolatrous life to serve the true and living God.

We need to make this kind of pledge to God. Come what may, we should follow the Lord's leading regardless to the pain, suffering, heartache, anguish, discouragement, persecution, adversity or sickness, poverty or wealth. We will not turn our backs on God; He promises that He will be with us even unto the end. We ought to be saying to God, regardless to what the difficulties are, Lord I will stick with you, and I'll stand by you. ***'For I am persuaded that neither death nor life, nor angels, nor principalities, nor powers, things present, nor things to come, nor height, nor depth, nor any creatures, shall be able to separate us from the love of God, which is in Christ Jesus our Lord'*** (Romans 8: 38-39).

When Naomi saw that Ruth had made up her mind and could not be persuaded otherwise, she stopped urging her to leave. By divine authority and appointment God had ordained Ruth to stay at Naomi's side, to support and under-gird her with the strength and stability that was necessary for her at this time. She was going to be the one to help her forget her pain.

They came to Bethlehem and the entire village was stirred at their arrival.

"Is it really Naomi?" the women asked.

She told them "Don't call me Naomi. Call me Mara," (Naomi means 'pleasant'; Mara means 'bitter') "for Almighty God has dealt me bitter blows. I went out full and the Lord has brought me home empty. Why should you call me Naomi when the Lord has turned His back on me and sent such calamity?" She was bitter because of all that happened to her; she felt God was unfair to her. She was experiencing pain and grief because her husband and sons had died. There was too much pain and as a result, the only way she thought she could have dealt with it, was to get bitter.

Back in Bethlehem they had to find a way to survive, so Ruth suggested that she would go into the fields of some kind gentleman to glean (gather) the free grain behind the reapers and Naomi agreed. She went into the fields of Boaz, the very wealthy relative of Naomi's husband. Boaz arrived from the city while she was there. After exchanging greetings with the reapers he said to his foreman after his eyes caught a glimpse of Ruth, "Hey, who's that girl over there?"

The foreman replied, "It's that girl from the land of Moab who came back with Naomi. She asked me this morning if she could pick up the grains dropped by the reapers, and she has been at it ever since except for a few minutes' rest over there in the shade." That was commendable, it showed her willingness to work, and this was not a lazy attitude at all but a new road to success. Was this going to be the beginning of a new life for Ruth, showing that she had the determination to turn over a new leaf for Naomi and herself, as she tried to push the past behind her? She needed this sort of moral support to give her an extra edge. She was humble also and did not think that the job was beneath her standard. Some folks like to start at the top, but note she was willing to start from the bottom and in due course of time God would elevate her.

Boaz went over and talked to her. "Listen, my child," he said, "Stay right here with us to glean; don't think of going to any other field. Stay right behind my women, not the workers; I have warned the young men not to bother you. When you are thirsty, go and help yourself to the water." Wow! For a stranger that's a good start: that was a polite invitation, this can help to raise her level of confidence. She knew now that she did not have to go anywhere else, she was welcomed there and would be looked after by all means. This is what God is saying to you as His child, stay right here in the kingdom of God, there is no need to go to anyone else. All that you need to fit you for life can be had right here in the Christian life. I would look after you. When you are thirsty I would give you drink.

She thanked him warmly. "How can you be so kind to me?" she asked. "You must know I am only a foreigner."

"Yes I know," Boaz replied, "and I also know about all the love and kindness you have shown your mother-in-law since the death of your husband, and how you left your father and mother in your own land and have come here to live among strangers. May the Lord of Israel, under whose wings you have come to take refuge, bless you for what you have done."

"Oh, thank you sir," she replied. "You are so good to me, and I'm not even one of your workers!"

At lunch time Boaz called to her, "Come and eat with us." So she sat with his reapers and they gave her more food than she could eat. When she went back to work Boaz told the young men to cut off some of the barley heads and purposely drop them for her to glean. She took the rest of the food home and all that she had gleaned back to Naomi.

Naomi, seeing what she brought home and found out that she went to the fields of Boaz was so excited and blessed the Lord for him and for being so kind to them. She explained to Ruth that he was a close relative of theirs. So Ruth gleaned with the workers until the end of the barley harvest, and then the wheat harvest also. God knew the heart of Ruth, He knew that she would be the one to work hard and bring the relief of financial frustration, loneliness, healing of emotional heartache and the pain of the past felt by Naomi and herself and would affect their life positively in time to come.

They were experiencing the favour of God on their lives thus man's favour would manifest itself. Sometimes the finite mind cannot predict and understand what God has in store for His children; all you need to do is trust Him in spite of your situation. You will wake up one morning and suddenly, He would change circumstances for you, by providing resources that you know nothing about, or others would be working for your benefit. You thought you were so insignificant but people of affluence and high esteem will start noticing you. He would even direct your steps where to go, because He knows where the provisions are. He would have men looking after your interest because of the plan he has in mind, just leave the past behind. Isaiah 43:18-19 (NIV) ***'Forget the former things; do not dwell on the past. See I am doing a new thing! Now it springs up; do you not perceive it? ...'***

One day Naomi said to Ruth, "My dear, isn't it time that I try to find a husband for you, and get you happily married again? The man I'm thinking of is Boaz! He has been so kind to us, and is a close relative. I happen to know that he will be winnowing barley tonight out on the threshing floor. Now do what I tell you – bathe and put on some perfume and some nice clothes and go on down to the threshing floor, but don't let him see you until he has finished his supper. Notice where he lies down to sleep; then go and lift the cover off his feet and lie down there, and he will tell you what to do concerning marriage."

The threshing floor was the place where the grain was separated from the harvest wheat. The wheat stalks were crushed either by hand or by oxen, and the valuable grains separated from the worthless chaff. The floor was made from rock or soil and was elevated where the wind could blow away the lighter chaff when the crushed wheat was thrown in the air. Boaz spent the night at the threshing floor either to prevent theft, or for his turn to thresh grain, which was normally done at nights.

Here is Naomi giving Ruth ideas of how she must go about getting Boaz, here is a woman with experience knowing that both of them went through some tough times of grief, moving from their locations during trying times of their lives, looking for a place of solitude. Naomi wanted to offer Ruth a chance for the better and she was prepared to let her do unprecedented things, which may not be considered as proper and correct but this was desperation. Could this be the break that they need or are they pushing their luck too far? The outcome depends on God, He is still in control.

Naomi's hopes are lifted by all this kindness by Boaz. Could this be kindness or true love? Let's find out. Boaz is not only wealthy but he could be enlisted as Ruth's 'kinsman-redeemer.' A kinsman-redeemer was a relative who has volunteered to take responsibility for the extended family. When a woman's husband died, the law (Deuteronomy 25:5-10) provided that she could marry the brother of her dead husband, but Naomi had no more sons. In this case, the nearest relative to the deceased husband could be the kinsman-redeemer and marry the widow. If he does not choose her then the next relative could take his place.

We have a kinsman-redeemer in Jesus Christ, who came down to earth as a man in order to save us. By his death on the cross, he redeemed us from sin and hopelessness and thereby purchased us to be His own possession. This guarantees our eternal inheritance.

As a foreigner, Ruth may have thought that Naomi's advice was odd but Ruth followed through regardless, because she knew Naomi was kind, trustworthy, and filled with moral integrity. You may know of a parent, older friend or relative who is always looking out for your best interest. Be willing to listen to the advice of those older and wiser than you are. The experience and knowledge of such a person can be valuable.

Ruth went down to the threshing floor that night and followed her mother-in-law's instructions. After Boaz had finished a good meal, he lay down very contentedly beside a heap of grain and went to sleep. Then Ruth came quietly and lifted the covering off his feet and lay there. Suddenly, around midnight, he awoke and sat up, startled. There was a woman lying at his feet! "Who are you?" he demanded.

"It's I, sir – Ruth," she replied. "Make me your wife according to God's law, for you are my close relative."

"Thank God for a girl like you!" he exclaimed. "For you are being kinder to Naomi now than even before. Naturally you'd prefer a younger man, even though poor, but you have put aside your personal desires so that you can give Naomi an heir by marrying me. Now don't worry about a thing, my child; I'll handle all the details, for everyone knows what a wonderful person you are. There is one problem though, it is true that I am a close relative but there is someone else who is more closely related to you than I am. Stay here tonight and I will talk to him in the morning and if he will marry you, fine; let him do his duty; but if he won't, then I will, I swear by Jehovah. Lie down until the morning." Imagine what Ruth's life would have been like had she ignored her mother-in-law.

So she lay at his feet until the morning and was up early, before daybreak, for he had said to her, "Don't let it be known that a woman was here at the threshing-floor." Boaz was an unselfish man. He had much to lose by honouring Ruth's request, especially since their first child would be Naomi's heir, not his. But Boaz focused on Ruth's virtuous qualities and was honoured that she had come to him, and God honoured him for this. He went to the market place and found the relative he had mentioned and spoke to him concerning Ruth whether he would purchase the lands from Naomi and marry Ruth so that she can have children to carry on her husband's name and inherit the land; or if not, he would do it himself.

The man replied "I cannot do it, for her son would become an heir to my property too, but you can do it." Then Boaz agreed to do it in the presence of all the witnesses and to the crowd standing around. So Boaz and Ruth were married and the Lord gave them a son. And the women of the city said to Naomi, "Bless the Lord who has given you this little grandson; may he be famous in Israel. May he restore your youth and take care of you in your old age; for he is the son of your daughter-in-law who loves you so much, and who has been kinder to you than seven sons!" And they named him Obed. He was the father of Jesse and the grandfather of King David; the line through which Jesus came.

Although Ruth belonged to a race often despised by Israel, God blessed her because of her faithfulness. He was also showing that the Gentile nations were engrafted in His plan of redemption and salvation. Ruth would have never guessed what was going to happen to her when she left Moab, but God orchestrated the whole plan and she followed each step of the way by trusting Him and leaving the past behind. Ruth worked hard to achieve her success, she had no idea what it would have turned out to be but she was willing to do it even for Naomi's sake. Because of her obedience, her life and legacy were significant even though she couldn't live to see all the results; to the extent that not just the story is recorded in the Bible but her name is the title of a book in the Bible.

Naomi said she was bitter when she came back from Moab, God used Ruth to quickly change things for her, from bitter she became better. This is not just a story of somebody's life that was turned around but, God used their adverse circumstances in preparation for the births of David and those in line for Jesus to be born, the promised Messiah. She could have continued to hold it against God and miss out on the blessings that He had in store for her.

We too must make our choices with God's eternal values in mind. You may be bitter about the past but leave it where it belongs in the past. You will not be able to take it with you into the future and be successful; get rid of it if you want to be better. Live in faithfulness to God, knowing that the significance of your life will extend beyond your lifetime. The rewards will outweigh any sacrifice you would have to make in your life time. When God takes something from your grasp, He is not punishing you but merely opening your hands to receive something better. The will of God will never take you where the grace of God will not protect you.

So don't let the misfortunes of your life cause you to get bitter, remain bitter and confine you to the past. The things you went through in life were not meant to hold you hostage and in bondage. God has something better for you, what you are holding on to cannot be measured by what is in store, so let it go. We cannot go through life without being hurt; it is the medium that God uses to bring us to the place where He wants us so that we can be of value to Him.

Being unwilling to forgive and holding on to bitterness will extend your pain, cause you to get hostile, affect your attitude and moods and as a result you would lose friends (Naomi still had her friends; Job had friends who lost confidence in him – they thought he had sinned, they were not true friends). Get rid of the bad memories of the past: they will kill you emotionally, spiritually and psychologically. Give them to God and forgive so that He can forgive you, or it will block your progress in life. Jesus says 'Your Heavenly Father will forgive you if you forgive those who sin against you; but if you refuse to forgive them, He will not forgive you' (Matthew 6:14-15 TLB). You are saying,

'This is a tough one.' Yes it is, but God will give you the grace to do it. Don't make the wounds of your past prevent you from being healed let them prepare you for the success of your future. Ruth and Naomi possessed some virtues that we need to have.

Perseverance and Endurance

If you are determined to be successful you have to learn to persevere and endure and not to quit. This simply means you have to complete all projects and assignments and God would know that you are an organized person and you are ready to move on. Don't sit back and wait for something to fall in your lap. This may mean getting involved in an activity while you are waiting for God's promise. Be assured that each day brings new challenges. Paul encountered shipwrecks, beaten so many times, imprisoned so many times, being in peril, yet he persevered. The key is remaining in the race, having patience to see what the outcome is going to bring you, ***"…let us run with patience the particular race that God has set before us. Keep your eyes on Jesus, our leader and instructor…"*** (Hebrews 12:1-2 TLB).

You need perseverance to turn your adversity into a win, win situation. Paul said "Now I want you to know, brothers, that what happened to me has really served to advance the gospel! (Philippians1:12 NIV). He found the grace that came from persevering during his trying times. God needs to see such virtues as your stability, strength and stamina; not a shortcut or quick-fix, nor release from growing pains. It would not take a single experience to get you where God wants you to go. It takes time to process and processing takes time to mature.

These experiences stretch us into our place of advancement, leaving us with stretch marks as in a pregnancy. Our lives will gradually take on a new phase and a new look, new meaning when eventually God will say, 'This is it.' That is when you are ready, becoming brighter and more beautiful as you shine more and more for Jesus. 'But as Christians we have no veil over our faces; we can be mirrors that brightly reflect the glory of the Lord. And as the Spirit of the Lord works within us, we become more and more like Him' (11 Corinthians 3:18TLB).

It is so easy to become weary and flunk the process before it is finished. It is so easy to get along with your spouse early in marriage, because it is fresh, exciting and you are energetic, full of life, so the task is much easier. Later on in life when age and years step in and your life is of a slower pace, the jobs look more difficult and the tasks feel like a mountain at times. We feel weary and can hardly cope with the challenges of life plus the calling of God is still to be answered. We wonder how we can ever fulfill it. That's when we need perseverance.

When Job was tested by Satan who took away his children and everything that he owned in one day; 'Job stood up and tore his robe in grief and fell down upon the ground before God. "I came naked from my mother's womb," he said "and I shall have nothing when I die. The Lord gave me everything I had, and they were His to take away. Blessed be the name of the Lord." In all of this, Job did not sin or revile God (Job 1: 20-22 TLB).

When Satan further afflicted his body with boils from head to foot; 'His wife said to him, "Are you still trying to be godly when God has done all this to you? Curse him and die." But he replied, "You talk like some heathen woman. What? Shall we receive only pleasant things from the hand of God and never anything unpleasant?" So in all this, Job said nothing wrong (Job 2:9-10 TLB).

'Then when Job prayed for his friends, the Lord restored his wealth and happiness! In fact the Lord gave him twice as much as before…So the Lord blessed Job at the end of his life more than at the beginning. God also gave him seven more sons and three daughters (Job 42:10-13 TLB).

We can never endure the things that Job went through, but in all of his difficulties and loss that he experienced he still praised God. He had an attitude of thanksgiving. He forgave his friends, he kept a level head, he knew and trusted God, and he maintained his worship and praise despite his misfortunes. He said, "Though He slay me, yet will I trust in Him: but I will maintain mine own ways before Him" (Job 13:15 KJV).

Do not make misfortune obscure your blessings for the future. Don't pine away and complain about all your losses but you need to count your blessings, which are so much more. Do not make a bad attitude deprive you of what God has in store for you, nor waiver in faith or stability. A thankful heart reflects inner strength and trust in God. God knows how to restore, so just be persistent in your perseverance and endurance. Let us not become ungrateful when situations take a down turn.

Paul says "Let us not be weary in doing good, for at the proper time we will reap a harvest if we do not give up" (Galatians 6:9 NIV). This is when we need our strength from God. Your best days are yet ahead. If your time was finished, God would have taken you but the fact that you are still here; this means there is still work for you to do. Don't be short- sighted; having no vision will make you miss the mission that God has for you. You just need a deeper commitment. There are times you are emotionally and physically drained because you are stuck somewhere and it is going to take an idea or a dream for you to persevere and have triumph.

James 1:2&3 says, 'Dear brothers, is your life full of difficulties and temptations? Then be happy, for when the way is rough, your patience has a chance to grow'. So let it develop and don't try to get yourself out of your problems. For when your patience is finally in full bloom, then you will be ready for anything, strong in character, full and complete mentally, spiritually and otherwise.

Endurance helps you to deal with a rebellious child even though the situation is unbearable and looks helpless. Endurance assists you on the road back to recovery from ill health, divorce, bad relationships, bankruptcy; steering your life back on track, picking up the pieces after each failure, returning back to school after teen-age pregnancy. It does not matter what the circumstances are, God will give you the grace to endure.

God is preparing you for success, so endure the hardships. It is the requirement for success in any field. Endurance is the vehicle that keeps you going, even when other vehicles have come to a dead end and it is also an anchor in the storms of life. Remember, God knows when to discontinue a trial; that is, when His purpose is fulfilled. Isaiah 43:5 says, 'Don't be afraid, for I am with you.' When you have a spirit of resilience and endurance, you would not be blown away or tossed by every wind of adversity. You would be like the tree planted by the river; your roots are embedded so deep that they are not easy to be up-rooted.

After times of trial Paul said (11Corinthians 12:9TLB), "I am glad to be a living demonstration of Christ's power, instead of showing off my own power and abilities." It is remaining faithful though we were blamed and slandered, not reviling or retaliating. We are hurt and are immersed in tears but still have the joy of the Lord for our strength to go on. Having needs in our lives, living on hand-outs but still meeting the needs of others worse than us; living in woes but the love of Jesus radiating and glowing on our faces and out of our mouths come forth springs of living water. Having endurance must be a commitment to achieving your life's dreams so that it becomes one of the priority of your life. 'You need to keep on patiently doing God's will if you want Him to do for you all that He has promised' (Hebrews 10:36TLB).

Chapter 12

PUSH – PRAY UNTIL SOMETHING HAPPENS

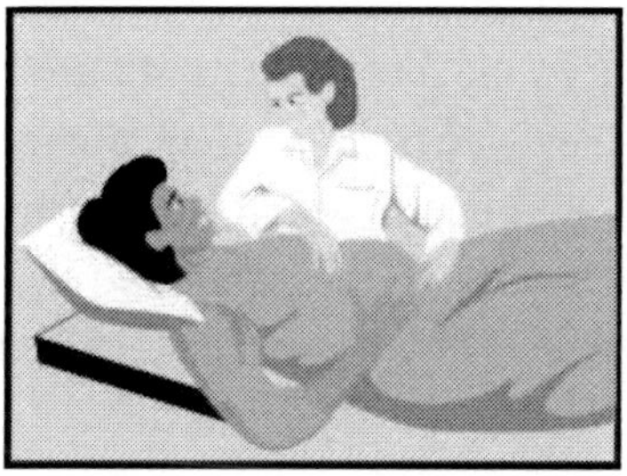

We began in Chapter 1 with the story of Hezekiah when Sennacherib, king of Assyria tried to challenge him to a battle. This is the message he sent to Isaiah (Isaiah 37: 3 TLB) saying: "This is a day of trouble and frustration and blasphemy; it is a serious time, as when a woman is heavy in labour trying to give birth, and the child does not come."

Isaiah replied in verse 4, "Tell King Hezekiah that the Lord says, 'Don't be disturbed by this speech from the servant of the king of Assyria, and his blasphemy. For a report from Assyria will reach the king that he will return to his own land, where I will have him killed.'"

The king of Assyria then received word that the prince of Ethiopia was leading an army against him (from the south). He sent word to King Hezekiah saying: "Don't let the God you trust fool you by promising that Jerusalem will not be captured by the king of Assyria! Just remember what has happened wherever the king of Assyria has gone, for they have crushed everyone who has opposed them. Do you think you will be different? …" He went on to name all the cities that were destroyed.

As soon as King Hezekiah read this letter, he went over to the Temple and spread it out before the Lord, and prayed, saying, "O Lord of Hosts, God of Israel enthroned above the cherubim, you alone are God of all the kingdoms of the earth. Listen as I plead; see me as I pray. Look at this letter from King Sennacherib, for he has mocked the Living God.

It is true, O Lord that the kings of Assyria have destroyed all those nations, just as the letter says, and thrown down their gods into the fire; for they weren't gods at all, but merely idols, carved by men from wood and stone. Of course the Assyrians could destroy them. O Lord our God, save us so that all the kingdoms of the earth will know that you are God, and you alone."

Then Isaiah sent a message to Hezekiah (Isaiah 37: 21&22 NIV) saying: "This is what the Lord, the God of Israel, says: Because you have prayed to me concerning the king of Assyria, this is the word the Lord has spoken against him: "The Virgin Daughter of Zion despises and mocks you. The daughter of Jerusalem tosses her head as you flee. Who is it you have insulted and blasphemed? Against whom have you raised your voice and lifted your eyes in pride? Against the Holy One of Israel?"

Come on Daughters of Zion; God delights in your gesture and mocks at Satan when he insults our God and the people of God. Come on men, let us pray. We are a team, we are in this together, PUSH – Pray Until Something Happens, so men and women would PUSH and give birth to the plan and purpose of God.

Isaiah 37: 33-38 (TLB) Therefore this is what the Lord says concerning the king of Assyria: "As for the king of Assyria, his armies shall not enter Jerusalem, nor shoot their arrows there, nor march outside its gates, nor build up an earthen bank against its walls. He will return to his own country by the road he came on, and will not enter this city, says the Lord. For my own honour I will defend it, and in memory of my servant David."

That night the Angel of the Lord went out to the camp of the Assyrians and killed 185,000 soldiers. When the living woke the next morning, all these lay dead before them. Then Sennacherib, returned to his own country, to Ninevah. And one day while he was worshipping in the temple of Nisroach his god, his sons Adrammelech and Sharezer killed him with their swords; then they escaped into the land of Ararat, and Esar-haddon his son became king.

What a victory! This is the God that we are serving, He has never changed. Hezekiah and his people did not even have to lift a hand to fight; the Angel of the Lord went to work and performed the task. He promised to fight all our battles for us and He is a winner all the time. He rolled back the waters of the Red Sea; also the waters of the river of Jordon, the walls of Jericho went tumbling down as the children of Israel shouted. He is the same God of yesterday as He is today. So place your confidence in your living God and PUSH, 'Now unto Him that is able to do exceeding abundantly above all that we ask or think, according to the power that works in us' (Ephesians 3:20 NKJV). We have the Holy Spirit dwelling within us; we just need to put that power to work, we can do it, so PUSH.

'…If you have faith like a grain of a mustard seed, you can say to this mountain, move from here… and it will move, and nothing will be impossible to you' (Matthew 17:20 AMP). For you shall decree a thing and it shall be established. Believe God for the things in your life that seem impossible, that mustard seed faith that has been deposited in you, put it to work. Just speak to your mountains of doubt, confusion, frustration, misery, strife, dispute, contention, manipulation and intimidation in the name of Jesus Christ, and by faith they shall disappear. You need to see a turn around in your life. Believe God and take Him at His word and PUSH.

Don't be afraid of the enemy; use your spiritual weapons and fight. 'For the Lord shall help me: therefore have I set my face like a flint, and I know that I shall not be ashamed,' (Isaiah 50:7). You may have struggled with some stuff in the past but you don't have to be ashamed. God will take care of it through the blood of Jesus Christ, so PUSH and come through with what the Lord has planned and designed for you.

This is an interesting story, so check this out.

A man was sleeping at night in his cabin when suddenly his room was filled with light, and God appeared. The Lord told the man that He had work for him to do, and showed him a large rock in front of his cabin. The Lord explained that the man was to push against the rock with all his might.

So this man did day after day. For many years he toiled from sun up to sun down, his shoulders set squarely against the cold, massive surface of the unmoving rock, pushing with all his might. Each night the man returned to his cabin sore and worn out, feeling that his whole day had been spent in vain.

Since the man was showing signs of discouragement, the adversary (Satan) decided to enter the picture by placing thoughts into the man's weary mind: "You have been pushing against that rock for a long time, and it hasn't moved." Thus, he gave the man the impression that the task was impossible and that he was a failure. These thoughts discouraged and disheartened the man. Satan said, "Why kill yourself over this? Just put in your time, giving just the minimum effort; and that will be good enough."

That's what the weary man planned to do, but decided to make it a matter of prayer and to take his troubled thoughts to the Lord.

"Lord he said, "I have laboured long and hard in your service, putting all my strength to do that which you have asked. Yet, after all this time, I have not even budged that rock by half millimeter. What is wrong? Why am I failing?"

The Lord responded compassionately, "My friend, when I asked you to serve Me and you accepted, I told you that your task was to push against the rock with all of your strength, which you have done. Never once did I mention to you that I expected you to move it…. Your task was to push.

And now you come to Me with your strength spent, thinking that you have failed. But, is that really so? Look at yourself. Your arms are strong and muscled, your back sinewy and brown; your hands are callused from constant pressure, your legs have become massive and hard through opposition, you have grown much, and your abilities now surpass that which you used to have. True, you haven't moved the rock. But your calling was to be obedient and to push and to exercise your faith and trust in My wisdom. That you have done. Now I, my friend, will move the rock."

There are times, when we hear a word from God, we tend to use our own intellect to decipher what He wants, and actually what God wants is just simple obedience and faith in Him. By all means, exercise the faith that moves mountains, but know that it is still God who moves mountains. You must have worked hard trying to be obedient to what God has asked you to do and you have not seen results, don't give up, God is looking on and He will soon reward your faithfulness. Or, you must have gone through some tough times and you have developed into a strong character with maturity of mind and spirit. You are not in a position to monitor your development but God has seen your efforts and is about to elevate you to a higher level. Again, don't give up but PUSH.

Don't be discouraged regardless of what the enemy says to you, God is about to step in, giving you words of commendation. When everything seems to go wrong, just PUSH! When the job gets you down, just PUSH! When people don't react the way you think they should, just PUSH! When your money is 'gone' and the bills are due, just PUSH! When people don't understand you, just PUSH! Both men and women are pregnant with the calling of God; this is not just a woman's affair so you just need to PUSH. There is so much pain and pressure but just PUSH.

You are not looking so attractive or handsome during this time of pregnancy, your face and nose is swollen, and you are oversized. You feel so sick sometimes but what you have growing inside of you is evidence of God's power to show to the world that you can make a difference with the calling that God has on your life. The way in which you take care of yourself taking proper vitamins, rest, appropriate exercise, visits to the doctor, will determine the outcome of the pregnancy. Likewise your attitude during these trying times, the time spent with God, reading His word, praying, witnessing, staying in subjection and submission, being mindful of contamination from the devil's vices and viruses, staying in the confines of God's will and taking care of yourself as you carry around God's promise inside of you would determine the outcome of your delivery.

You may be experiencing morning sickness, you feel so nauseated at times. Each time you smell the environment around you or when things are not going right at home you want to vomit because it makes you sick. The office gossip upsets you, the stench of bad living in your community, the violence, crime, and drugs, drop-out in society, teenage pregnancies get to you. There is also the question of you not having the powerful witness as a Christian in your community, which you ought to have, becomes a burden to you. You are pregnant with the calling of God. You know that God is calling you to make a difference but you are afraid to answer that call and take your rightful place. You are timid and fearful of handling your responsibility, and what people would say about you, but you were called to make a difference, so speak or scream out when you feel the pain of ills and wrongs. PUSH so that you can make an impact; when the mid-wife says PUSH, you have to PUSH.

Your pregnancy has just begun and you have had some bad feelings and experiences, 'by bringing up your guts' to the wrong church people, who just could not understand your passion, or who could not stand you in the first place. The result was that they ended up ill-speaking you, and now you are discouraged, afraid to go on further to full term and come to your prophetic fulfillment. God will give you the endurance to go on. For the Lord God is your sun and shield: He will give grace and glory, no good thing will He withhold from those who walk uprightly (Psalm 84:11 KJV). Don't abort your dreams, there is too much at stake, you have come too far to give up now. God will strengthen you, so go on to full term.

The 'Labour Pains' that you have been feeling are to bring you into your destiny, so PUSH in order to deliver and bring forth that which God has deposited within you. You may be in a situation where you feel hopeless and helpless; you have to PUSH yourself out of it. Feel the intensity of 'Labour Pains' and you know it is time that you deliver. You may be trapped in a situation, no matter what it is, come on give it a PUSH. Pray for God's strength and PUSH. God is mighty and strong and ready to deliver you from whatever you are going through. He would not allow the devil to hold you in bondage and captivity as long as you are ready to PUSH and come through.

When you are expecting to have a child you would make proper provisions and preparations: have the necessary equipment like a cot, clothes, blankets, bottles and whatever is required for when the baby arrives. If you do not have what is necessary then it means that you are not prepared for delivering a baby. Even so, you would not be ready for your dreams to come forth if you are not prepared. When God gives you a vision of what you are going to do, then it is your responsibility to prepare by way of the forecast. For those of you who have been planning and preparing then go ahead and PUSH. When everything is in place for your delivery, PUSH, it will be worth it all, when you have come through.

'Labour Pains' vary in length. Some people go into labour for some hours and some go for days. Some 'Labour Pains' vary also in intensity. Regardless to your period or intensity, do not give up, don't just keep on calling for the nurse, your husband, wife, mother, father or whoever, for help. Call upon your God, He is EL-SHADDAI – God Almighty (the all sufficient mighty One), JEHOVAH-JIREH – the Lord will provide (the Lord will foresee and provide), JEHOVAH-ROPHE – the Lord that heals (our healer, spiritually and physically), JEHOVAH-ROHI – the Lord is my Shepherd (the Shepherd tenderly provides and guides), JEHOVAH-SHAMMAH – the Lord is There… (The eternal presence of the Holy One). Give praise, honour and glory despite the pain, for you will come forth.

God is inducing labour, hence the urgency of the time. The contractions are increasing and the time span between each one is getting less. If you find that you can't cry then, you need to groan, and PUSH and come forth. Let the devil see you can do it. You are not afraid of him. Remember the struggle you are in, is not yours, it belongs to God, so give it to Him. He will fight your battle for you, all you need to do is PUSH. Get desperate and violent. The kingdom of God suffers violence but the violent takes it by force (Matthew 11: 12), come forth with your dreams.

God has planted some seeds in your life; they have germinated and grown with time. You did not even notice it, but take a good look and have an introspection at where the Lord has taken you from and where you are now. Let someone know, not because they did not see the fruits, it did not mean that you were not blooming; but your time of fruition is coming as God is inducing 'Labour Pains'. So PUSH, so that you can have an off-spring;

this is your season of bearing fruit. Folks may have thought that you were barren and that you could not bear fruit. Come on, show them what God has been doing in your life, the evidence and manifestation of production is soon to come forth, so PUSH.

Let the nurse or mid-wife know that she need not give up on you because you are coming through soon. When people see you a while from now they will not be able to recognize you because you would not be blotted with pride, malice, jealousy or any such sins of the flesh because you are going to PUSH and get rid of them. You would not be wearing any over-sized clothes; you would be all dressed up in royal robes of righteousness. You could say to folks if they gave you their weird look, "Don't hate me, just celebrate with me. You don't know what I have been through to get here, but thank God I've made it."

You may have fallen from grace so many times. God picked you up and dusted you off. Thank God you did not have a miscarriage, you are still carrying the plan of God. He loves you too much to let you stay down. You are determined now that you will not slip and fall again; you are going full term by the grace of God. That which you are carrying is so precious; you can't afford to lose it. When Elizabeth heard the greeting from Mary, her baby inside her leaped, she was filled with the Holy Ghost and spoke with a loud voice … Let the Holy Ghost speak from within you. For out of your belly shall flow rivers of living water, let it flow as you PUSH. 'If they fall it isn't fatal, for the Lord holds them with his hand' (Psalm 37:24TLB).

Do you know what your fetus is comprised of? It involves your talents, abilities, assignments, experiences, gifts, ambitions, purposes, goals, desires, aims, the stamina which in time you have developed, the spine, muscles and capabilities they were developed with hard work, maturity, readiness, correct focus. You can PUSH, 'No weapon that is formed against you will prosper, and every tongue that shall rise against you in judgment you shall condemn. This is the heritage of the servants of the Lord…' (Isaiah 54: 17KJV). No matter what folks say or try to do it cannot stand, just use your legal right and authority that God has equipped you with and cast out, condemn, defy and deny the works of the enemy in the name of Jesus and PUSH.

When you are committed to bring forth what God has placed within you, you will have to PUSH against everything everybody ever did to you or said about you. Now God will help you to bring it out, but it's up to you to PUSH. In fact it will not happen to you if you don't. You will have to PUSH against Satanic attacks in all their devious and debilitating forms; such as bad experiences, low self-esteem and feelings of worthlessness. The devil may have spent years pushing you aside, pulling you back and putting you down, but today God is saying to you, "I want to open you up, I want to empower you, to give birth to what I have placed and developed within you."

When a baby is born everything in the family changes. The same is true for you. When you give birth to what God has placed within you, everything in your life will be affected. God's blessing will overflow and touch every area of your existence. So come on PUSH for changes are about to take place, new dreams, new visions and destiny is about to come forth.

You will not experience a still-born, because you are protected and taken care of by the Triune Being. When the fullness of time was come Jesus was born of a Virgin Mary. When the fullness of time is come you too will come forth. Do not make adversities, cares, strife, turmoil, pressures of life, difficulties, or hunger make you abort the plan of God. It has cost you so much already: the loss of appetite, sleeplessness, discomfort, sacrifices, you have been criticized, slandered, talked down to, pressured but don't give up the struggle. You have come thus far by faith, leaning on the arms of the everlasting Father. Weeping may endure for the night but joy cometh in the morning. If you can only see what you will bring forth, you will never abort or terminate the plan of God. You have come too far to destroy your dream.

You may be asking, 'When do I PUSH?' Whenever you feel the urgency, the discomfort of what is happening around you or in life, when situations are unbearable, even when there is no mid-wife around, just PUSH. There are some who would like to take the drug Epidural, so that they would not have to feel the pain, but no pain, no gain. It is an established fact that the drug has an after effect that lasts for years but 'Labour Pains' would not last forever. Come on, you just need to 'Put on the whole armour of God, that you may be able to stand against the wiles of the devil. For you are not wrestling against flesh and blood but against principalities and powers, against the rulers of darkness of this world, against spiritual wickedness in high places' (Ephesians 6:12 KJV). Come on just PUSH.

There are some folks who would like to have babies but do not want to get pregnant. This simply means they would like to have the blessings that God has in store for them but they do not want to go through the channel that He would use to bring them to that time and place of delivery. In other words, they are not prepared to be obedient to His will. They do not want the trials and the pain, they want the nice times and pleasures of the world. Who has given you the talent and the gift to do what others find difficult or impossible? 'Remember, it is the Lord your God, who gives you power to succeed in life' (Deut. 8: 18 AMP). The pain would not kill you, it was not meant to destroy you either, and it is only for a time.

There is a connection between your blessing and the purpose of God in your life. You didn't have God's favour because of the family you came from, but He has a bigger plan down the road. Do not run from the purpose, or beat your chest, or hoard everything for yourself but extend God's kingdom with it. The increased finances, good health, places of affluence and influence with people in authority, are God's gift for you to do God's will. Many times people take God's blessings and turn their back on Him, or don't want to align themselves with God's people or His plans. That is when the enemy will pull you down because he is after your **provision, position, possession and purpose**. Don't compromise your stand and your faith in God because the **pregnancy** and the **pain** comes in one package, so take it and PUSH. Come on PUSH and press towards the prize of the high calling of God in Christ Jesus.

When you are pregnant your health can be challenged. The woman with the issue of blood was sick for twelve years and had gone to all the doctors for help but no one could help her. That day she came to see Jesus, she was determined and made up her mind that despite the crowd she was going to press her way through. She thought, if only I could touch the hem of Jesus' garment I can be made whole, so she pressed and she pressed, or she pushed and she pushed until she saw the hem of His garment and she touched it and she was made whole. If you are sick in your body, you just need to PUSH and PUSH and you too can be made whole. He was wounded for our transgressions and He was bruised for our iniquities: the chastisement of our peace was upon Him; and with His (Jesus') stripes you are healed (Isaiah 53:5).

Are you challenged financially during this time of pregnancy; because of the economic crisis in your country you have lost your job? In God's economy there is no melt down. Isaac sowed in the time of famine and received one hundred fold blessing. Give to the work of God, give to charitable organizations, and give to those who are in need. If you do, God will open up the windows of heaven for you and pour out a blessing so great you won't have room enough to take it in! (Malachi 3:10). So PUSH to receive your financial blessings from God. Don't complain and murmur like the children of Israel but give God thanks and

He will bless you. 'But my God shall supply all your need according to His riches in glory by Christ Jesus' (Philippians 4:19).

Your legs may be in stirrups now and you have been exposed so that you can come forth. This is not indecent exposure in a negative sense but God is about to expose your faithfulness, your fine character, your morale, the things that you have been doing under cover, those deeds which were done privately for Him, the actions behind the scenes that nobody noticed or cared about, your name was seldom mentioned. God is about to elevate you, exposing you and bring you to the forefront, because of your integrity and credibility. You have given your time, efforts and money with much sacrifice and not making an open show of it. He is about to show you off and bring you from your secret place. 'But when you do a kindness to someone, do it secretly; don't tell your left hand what your right hand is doing. And your Father who knows all secrets will reward you openly' (Matthew 6:3-4), so PUSH.

Now the pain has become more intense and the nurse thinks that you are about time to come forth because you are dilating, so she says PUSH but you cannot come forth, so you need further help. A surgeon will perform a cesarean section, using his surgical instruments and inserting a cut with surgical knife. God's Word is sharper than a surgeon's scalpel, cutting through everything, whether doubt or fear, it is a powerful tool, defeating every plan and strategy of the enemy that may hinder and prevent the process of you coming forth.

As the surgeon's scalpel cuts us and exposes that which is inside, he not only takes out the baby out of the womb, he also takes out that which is attached; the extended umbilical cord, the placenta, which was offering protection, and he discards these, no longer necessary. In the same manner, God's word will get rid of the unwanted stuff like complacency, doubt, fear, double-mindedness, lack of faith; as the word of God takes effect. 'For whatever God says to us is full of living power: it is sharper than the sharpest dagger, cutting swift and deep into our innermost thoughts and desires with all their parts, exposing us for what we really are' (Hebrews 4:12).

God is the one who determines the sex and genes of your baby as long as the pregnancy is by natural conception. You cannot dictate the sex of your child; you just have to accept it. In like manner, as long your life is placed in God's hand and He dictates His will, He is the one who chooses your destiny, where you go and when, what you do and how. Have you wondered how you ended up being an engineer when you wanted to be a doctor, or a police officer instead of a businessman? It is because God was directing your calling and He knows what your purpose here is on earth, so PUSH.

In Revelation 12, a great pageant appeared in heaven, portraying things to come. John the revelator said he saw a woman clothed with the sun, with the moon beneath her feet, and a crown of twelve stars on her head. She was pregnant and screamed in the pain of her labour, awaiting her delivery. Suddenly a red Dragon appeared, with seven heads and ten horns, and seven crowns on his head. His tail drew along behind him a third of the stars, which he plunged to the earth. He stood before the woman as she was about to give birth to her child, ready to eat the baby as soon as it was born. She gave birth to a boy who was to rule all nations with a heavy hand, and he was caught up to God and to his throne. The woman fled into the wilderness, where God had prepared a place for her, to take care of her for 1,260 days.

The woman represents God's faithful people who have been awaiting the Messiah; the twelve stars represent the tribes of Israel. Satan wanted to kill Jesus at birth but Jesus had a purpose: why? He came to save the people from their sins. Satan would want to kill our babies at birth also so that they would not fulfill the plan of God for their lives. There was war in heaven; Michael and the angels under his command fought the Dragon and his hosts of fallen angels. The dragon lost the battle and was forced from heaven. This great dragon – the ancient serpent called the devil or Satan, the one deceiving the whole world – was thrown down into the earth with all his army.

Then John said he heard a loud voice shouting across the heavens, "It has happened at last! God's salvation and the power and the rule, and the authority of His Christ are finally here; for the Accuser of our brothers has been thrown down from heaven onto earth. He accused them day and night before our God. They defeated him by the blood of the Lamb, and by their testimony; for they did not love their lives but laid them down for him.

Rejoice, O heavens! You citizens of heaven, rejoice! Be glad! But woe to you people of the world, for the devil has come down to you in great anger, knowing that he has little time." And the dragon found himself cast down to earth; he persecuted the woman who had given birth to the child. But she was given two wings like those of a great eagle, to fly into the wilderness to the place prepared for her, where she was cared for and protected from the serpent, the Dragon, for three and a half years.

From the serpent's mouth a vast flood of water gushed out and swept toward the woman in an effort to get rid of her; but the earth helped her by opening its mouth and swallowing the flood. Then the furious Dragon set out to attack her children – all who were keeping God's commandments and confessing that they belong to Jesus. He stood waiting on an ocean beach.

As this drama unfolds it shows clearly how Satan tried to get at Jesus but he could not. He tried to get at the woman who gave birth but she was protected and when he could not get at her he went after her children. Thank God for those who overcame by the power of the blood and by the words of their testimony. Satan would continue to test you and try you, want to kill you, but you are protected by the blood of Jesus, so stay firm, hold on to God's plan for your life and don't lose faith or sight of your goal. Stay in God's control, stay in the ark of safety, under God's covering – His everlasting arms. 'He that dwells in the secret place of the most High shall abide under the shadow of the Almighty. I will say of the Lord, He is my refuge and my fortress: my God, in Him will I trust' (Psalm 91:1-2 KJV).

You have been abused and accused yes, but PUSH, battered and bruised yes, but PUSH, pushed and shoved yes, but PUSH. They said you would not amount to anything but still PUSH, because God is about to open your door of destiny and opportunity and close those of impossibilities and misfortunes. Make sense of your pain because you are not going through this for nothing, see the good in it, God's grace is going to allow you to get ahead again, to live life in its fullness again. 'These troubles and sufferings of ours are, after all, quite small and won't last very long. Yet this short time of distress will result in God's richest blessing upon us forever and ever!' (2Corinthians 4:17 TLB).

Position yourself because these last contractions would be the hottest and fastest but when it is finished you would have given birth to your dreams. Do not make anything in the past stand in your way now. You have to go forward; you cannot relinquish your efforts now. Your breathing has to be right. With the power of the Holy Spirit energizing you, you have to be determined because you have a vision of what is coming forth and it looks good. It is too late to be discouraged and frustrated, or to give up. This is your defining moment, this is what you have waited so long for, and just one last PUSH will do it. When it hurts you so badly give your pain to Jesus. "Lord have mercy!" you scream, "This is the hottest pain I ever feel, help me Jesus or I would die, I can't bear this any more!" Then… Alas! Congratulations!

Here's an announcement, it's over! You have made it! It is here! It has happened! You have done it! Hallelujah! You may have come forth for this is your dream and your vision that you have given birth to! "Yet sooner is Zion in labour than she gives birth to her children. Do I bring to the moment of birth and not give delivery?" says the Lord. "Do I close up the womb when I bring to delivery?" says the Lord your God (Isaiah 66:8 NIV). God is about to move you into new arenas, and to other levels of spiritual power, bigger and better dimensions. You will see more and more manifestations of His power: new doors are going to be opened, so forget your past pain and start praising, just celebrate because there are other dreams and visions that are about to come forth, while you continue to fulfill your destiny and purpose in this life. Give the Lord a mighty shout of Praise, because he accomplishes it for you.

'So now, since we have been made right in God's sight by faith in his promises, we can have real peace with him because of what Jesus Christ our Lord has done for us. For because of our faith, He has brought us into this place of highest privilege where we now stand, and we confidently and joyfully look forward to actually becoming all that God has had in mind for us to be.

We can rejoice, too, when we run into problems and trials for we know that they are good for us: they help us learn to be patient. And patience develops strength of character in us and help us trust God more each time we use it, until finally our hope and faith are strong and steady' (Romans 5:1-4 TLB).

Let us give God all the praise and thanks for bringing us through our trials, for He is the king of glory. He is ELOHIM, the one that has created us by His great power. He is the great God of the universe and he has chosen to give us the Bible, full of blessed promises to live by. Thank you, ELOHIM, for writing down your covenant in the Holy Scriptures. Thank you for loving us so much that you gave us the precious covenant of the cross and allowed Jesus Christ to give His life as a sacrifice on it so that we can be redeemed and have new purposes in life. Thank you Holy Spirit for bringing us to Jesus Christ, for you lead and guide us into all truth. We worship and adore the Triune Being.

Let us conclude with this writing from a young friend, Demol James, who has termed himself as the Black Panther. Here it comes:

My New Friend

I thank the Lord for today, for the deliverance that has been granted to me through faith. The life of the Black Panther has been a battle of physical and mental fights but through it all, perseverance overcame fear, guilt and ignorance. The time has come to elevate myself from the negative attitude that has locked me away in my past of hardship and disappointments. I always asked the question, how can I persevere and overcome this mental battle? The answer to this question was given to me through a friend. This friend I met made me comfortable so I started to talk to him about my problems and I then realized that He has all the answers to fill my heart with positive vibrations giving me complete deliverance and peace from anxiety and confusion. By now I know you are curious to know about this friend that is helping me with my transformation.

My friend is perfect and has all the answers to my problems and shows me the direct path to prosperity and that is not only half of what He is. There is only one person who always sees me when I cry and notices when my day is filled with depression and He is Jesus Christ. Jesus Christ made me a better person and a more positive individual. He made my dark soul shine out and everyone noticed how extraordinary our new friendship was, for there is no fear in love, for perfect love cast away fear, for fear has torment. He has given me hope that dispels doubt and grief, peace that surpasses all understanding, joy unspeakable and full of glory, rivers of joy that flood my soul and I am drinking from a stream that never runs dry. All this comes from my new friend, Christ Jesus, just trust Him today, He will not fail you.

THE END

ABOUT THE AUTHOR OF 'LABOUR PAINS'

Mrs. Kay Blugh Gaymes has spent her life in the church, and has served in the capacity as Sunday school teacher, youth leader, young women coordinator, worship leader, evangelist and preacher. She has also spearheaded women's conferences as facilitator and speaker. She has spoken in churches in the United Kingdom and the United States.

She is a firm believer that prayers and the Word are responsible for the success of her life as the wife of a Pastor and the mother of four children. Despite her busy schedule she holds a Certificate in Public Administration (University of the West Indies Mona, Jamaica); an Executive Diploma in Management (University of the West Indies Cave Hill, Barbados); a Master in Business Administration (Leicester University, UK). She had thirty years experience in Public Service of St. Vincent and the Grenadines. These disciplines are just God's medium of opening doors for her to walk through to fulfill His calling.

Gaymes takes the calling of God very seriously, and feels that she ought to obey the prophetic utterances spoken over her life. Nothing debars her from interfacing with the poor and down trodden; she feels that regardless of who we are, we need inspiration and encouragement for the rough and bumpy rides on life's journey. She has reached out to many broken lives and hurting people in many ways.

She believes that the power of God is not being demonstrated in it's fullness to bring deliverance to lives especially to young people who are under attack from the enemy, which has affected their lives negatively, causing them to miss their calling in God. She is desirous to see a break through in various ways in the Body of Christ.

kayblughgaymes@yahoo.com
website address: wwwlabourpains.org

Remember you can fulfill God's plan for life,
all you need to do is to trust God with your whole heart,
and He will direct your steps,
for the steps of a good man are ordered by the Lord.